1 MONTH OF
FREE
READING

at
www.ForgottenBooks.com

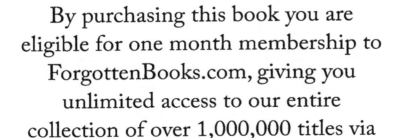

By purchasing this book you are eligible for one month membership to ForgottenBooks.com, giving you unlimited access to our entire collection of over 1,000,000 titles via our web site and mobile apps.

To claim your free month visit:
www.forgottenbooks.com/free1121757

ISBN 978-0-331-42251-1
PIBN 11121757

This book is a reproduction of an important historical work. Forgotten Books uses state-of-the-art technology to digitally reconstruct the work, preserving the original format whilst repairing imperfections present in the aged copy. In rare cases, an imperfection in the original, such as a blemish or missing page, may be replicated in our edition. We do, however, repair the vast majority of imperfections successfully; any imperfections that remain are intentionally left to preserve the state of such historical works.

The Good Neighbor Council

By David Gergen, *Administrative Assistant*
North Carolina Good Neighbor Council

As events of the summer and fall have dispelled hopes of achieving an early settlement to the civil rights crisis in this country, many North Carolinians have begun to ask themselves about their future.

The political campaigns, the backlash, the riots, bloodshed, and the fragmentation of national Negro leadership have all injected much uncertainty into considerations. They have also demonstrated, however, that the present civil rights legislation, as significant and far-reaching as it may be, has not rendered a full solution. The fires of discontent burn fiercely and will continue to lick at the nation's social and economic structure until something more is done.

In response, North Carolinians are asking how a peace can be found which is both just and acceptable. What should our goals now be and how can we reach them in an orderly fashion? How much are our people prepared to support? How can additional support be won? In short, where do we go from here?

During the past twenty-two months, Governor Terry Sanford and the leaders of many communities have been convinced that the areas in which the most constructive and beneficial progress can be made are education and employment. They feel that by working together to improve the education and expand the job opportunities of all citizens, we can lift both our moral and economic horizons.

Their beliefs are expressed through their support of the North Carolina Good Neighbor program. Governor Sanford initiated the program in January, 1963, when he announced formation of a State Good Neighbor Council. This group, he said, had a two-fold mission of encouraging employment of qualified people without regard to race and urging youth to become better trained and qualified for employment. Efforts were to be voluntary and of a low-pressure sort. Since the Governor's announcement, forty-seven communities have established local Good Neighbor councils or have adopted the mission of the Good Neighbor program as a major concern of their human relations

committee. These groups have a total membership of some 750, all of whom are men and women of stature.

In the short time that they have been formed, the councils have recorded many important breakthroughs. For the most part, they have been active organizations, more interested in concrete changes than talk and tokenism. Their work has continued unabated since passage of the equal employment sections of the Civil Rights Act, for they believe that much has to be done at the local level before the provisions can be meaningful.

Now, as North Carolinians consider the future, the experiences of the Good Neighbor program may provide some valuable lessons. The approaches taken by various groups, the insights gained, and the successes achieved should be instructive for all concerned with genuine, long-range solutions and with the needs and potentialities of State and local action.

In this article, we shall look first at the Negro and the economy as they are seen by the leaders of the Good Neighbor program. Having placed the problems in this perspective, we can turn to a description of the activities of State and local groups and the experiences of major employers. Finally, we can examine the conclusions which have been drawn by the program leadership.

The Negro and the North Carolina Economy

Soon after embarking upon their activities, many participants in the Good Neighbor program found that the problems with which they were dealing were more difficult and deep-rooted than ever imagined. The notion of traditional jobs, the concept of a cycle of poverty, the fear of change—these were all familiar. But for some participants, the extent of the poverty and poor education, the manner in which discrimination had seared the character of the Negro and built walls between the races, the depth of resentments, and the complex relationship between all aspects of a solution—these were sobering revelations.

Some grasp of the problems can be obtained by viewing the North Carolina Negro as he exists in the census books, economic charts, and other records. His most salient statistical features form an interesting pattern:

● Some 70 percent of the Negro families in North Carolina had incomes of less than $3,000 in 1959, compared to 29 percent of the whites. A family with less than $3,000 is generally considered poverty-stricken.

● The median income of Negro families was $1,922 in 1959, which was approximately four-tenths the size of the median income of white families.

● While Negro family income increased between 1949 and 1959, the Negro did not fully share in the new abundance and he consequently lost ground relative to the white; the Negro median fell from 48% of the white family median in 1949 to 43% in 1959.

• The dollar gap between white and Negro median family income in North Carolina increased from $1,159 to $2,596 in the 1949-59 period.

• The unemployment rate among Negroes has been at least twice as high as the rate among whites since 1951.

• Some 8.4% of Negro workers were in white collar, clerical, or sales jobs in 1959, compared to 36.6% of whites.

• The Negro male with one to three years of college earned less in 1959 than the white male with an elementary education (eight years), while the Negro college graduate earned less than the white high school graduate.

• Half of the Negroes above 25 years of age in 1960 had less than seven years of schooling, compared to 9.8 years for whites.

• Of those Negroes scheduled to complete their high school education in 1960, some 61% had dropped out before graduation, compared to 46% of the white students.

• Negro enrollment in the State's Industrial Education Centers has also been poor, generally running 10% or less of the total enrollment.

• On the other hand, of the net migration of 207,000 Negroes from North Carolina between 1950 and 1960, the highest rates of migration were among the young and best educated.

• Largely because of the migration, the number of Negro college graduates 25 years old or older living in North Carolina increased from 12,400 to only 17,400 from 1950 to 1960, while the comparable number of whites jumped from 89,000 to 127,400. Negro colleges in this State graduate several thousand a year.

The statistics could run on endlessly, but the main outlines of the average Negro's life in North Carolina should already be clear. It is a tale for which our society has devised many labels: substandard housing, cultural deprivation, inadequate schooling, school drop-out, juvenile delinquency, unemployment, underemployment, welfare, etc.

Whites can never fully understand the psychological implications, but they often find it illuminating to compare their own lives with the average Negro's life. The Negro child, growing up in a culture of poverty, generally enters school a year or two behind whites in aptitude testing. The "pass-along" system in some Negro schools allows the child to continue his education until age 16 without learning how to read or write. By this time, if he can read, the youth realizes that the curriculum in his school, particularly in the vocational areas, may be limited, that his teaching may be inferior, and that even if he finishes high school, his employment opportunities will not be much improved. Aspirations destroyed, many soon quit. Those who finish in a predominantly Negro school, according to the Secretary of Labor's 1964 Manpower Report, may be as many as two years behind their white counterparts. This system is usually continued well into college or technical training. As a result, the Negro taking a pre-employment test in North Carolina often does relatively poorly despite the fact that he may have had as many years of formal education and that he may originally have had the same potential as the white taking the test. Few men are ever born who can surmount all of these obstacles. The majority in years past have had little chance of doing anything more than perpetuating the system.

As these terms would suggest, the Negro cannot be understood apart from the society in which he lives. Indeed, he is inextricably bound to the State's socio-economic structure and shares its fate. If the economy falters, he falters, and if he fails to prosper, the economy also fails. White standards of living may rise more rapidly than Negro standards, but their actual rate of increase will always be far below their potential rate as long as one-quarter of the population fails to prosper.

David Gergen, right, hands a report to Good Neighbor Chairman D. S. Coltrane. At center is Dr. James T. Taylor, vice-chairman, of the Council. Gergen is administrative assistant to Coltrane and author of this article.

This proposition can perhaps be examined from two views. The first is to assume that we preserve the economic and educational system of recent years, if that is possible. In this case, North Carolina would continue to pay at least the same high costs which she now pays for the present system. Today's educated Negro finds economic opportunities in the North and West more inviting than in the South and quickly migrates. As a result, taxpayers are making an investment in his education in North Carolina which pays off in other states. In some instances, the State pays twice, for the relatives left behind are poorly educated and cannot easily support themselves or the economy. A year ago a popular newspaper columnist wrote of a Negro family in which seven children were educated in North Carolina and then left the State for productive work elsewhere, while an eighth child and the parents stayed behind on the welfare rolls. Yet these are only the direct, easily identifiable costs. Others more subtle and more difficult to calculate result from underemployment, welfare benefits, juvenile correction, and more recently, the demonstrations. The President's Council of Economic Advisers asserted in 1962 that because of racial discrimination, the nation's economy is losing between $13 and $17 billion a year in national income. Upon the basis of these figures, the South's annual loss can be conservatively pegged at $5-6 billion.

Moreover, the costs of this system are likely to grow much higher in the future. More than half of the Negro population in North Carolina is now below 20 years of age. If these people continue to drop out of school at a 61% rate, they will present an overwhelming unemployment problem, for they will be unable to find jobs in an economy which is rapidly requiring skills of even its lowest-paid employees. Unemployment among Negro youth, it may be noted, reached 25% on a nation-wide basis dur-

2

ing the summer and was considered a major factor in the northeastern riots. Thus, aside from the moral and international considerations, the racial question is really whether North Carolina can afford to pay the costs of wasted manpower and unprofitable investments.

As an alternative, the State might try to educate all of its available manpower and to employ on a merit basis. This approach, while challenging, nevertheless offers far more hope for the future, in the opinion of the Good Neighbor program leadership. By this method, we would be able to take advantage of the best skills within our society and to turn our present losses into substantial gains.

The businessman might well ask whether the State has a sufficient number of jobs to begin this change. Latest figures from the Employment Security Commission headquarters in Raleigh indicate that at a time when we have 84,000 people unemployed, we also have at least 10,000-15,000 jobs which are unfilled in North Carolina, primarily because employers cannot find qualified personnel. Almost all of these jobs are in the professional, skilled and clerical categories. More importantly, the demand in these areas promises to grow rapidly in coming years. A study in 1961 by the Employment Security Commission found that by 1966, industries already in the State would require an additional 30,000 skilled workers and 8,000 technicians. Another survey, conducted in 1963, indicated that by the fall of 1966, North Carolina would have an additional 17,000 openings in the trade area, 4,000 in finance, 4,500 in insurance, and 2,000 in service. A third study, which was also undertaken by the ESC in the fall of 1963, found that manpower needs in selected medical and health service occupations would reach 11,500 by the end of 1966. If North Carolina continues to train workers at its present rate, shortages will exist in all of these fields. Our training shortages in the technician field alone are now piling up at the rate of 800 jobs a year. Hence there are not only potentialities, but dramatic need for trained personnel of both races.

Some might still wonder whether, if we trained all of our people, we might have a surplus of trained workers. That's partly true, but should cause little concern. One need only remember that just as there is a cycle of poverty, there is also a cycle of prosperity. The question, from the point of view of the Good Neighbor program, is how to break into that second circle. For a State which stands 11th in the nation in population and 43rd in per capita income, one of the first and most important steps is to make better use of its available manpower. Other steps, as populous, developing countries across the globe are proclaiming, may well lie in increased investment and a spirit of innovation. If we can break into the charmed cycle, we should have little worry about a surplus of trained workers, for prosperity even in an automated age usually generates a strong demand for more workers.

Establishment of the Good Neighbor Program

After considering these and other ideas, Governor Sanford began to lay formal groundwork for the Good Neighbor program in November, 1962, when he discussed his ideas with leading whites and Negroes who had been invited to a breakfast in Raleigh. Encouraged by their response, he sought out several citizens for the State Council membership in late December. He could then have announced the establishment of the group in a brief statement, but he decided that more forthright leadership was necessary. Seizing an opportune moment—a gathering of the North Carolina Press Association in Chapel Hill—he coupled his report on the Council with one of the boldest statements on civil rights ever made by a Southern governor.

"Now is a time not merely to look back to freedom, but forward to the fulfillment of its meaning," he said. "Despite great progress, the Negro's opportunity to obtain a good job has not been achieved in most places across the country. Reluctance to accept the Negro in employment is the greatest single block to his continued progress and to the full use of the human potential of the Nation and its States.

"The time has come for American citizens to give up this reluctance, to quit unfair discriminations, and to give the Negro a full chance to earn a decent living for his family and to contribute to higher standards for himself and all men.

"We cannot rely on law alone in this matter because much depends upon its administration and upon each individual's sense of fair play . . .

"We can do this. We should do this. We will do it because we are concerned with the problems and the welfare of our neighbors. We will do it because our economy cannot afford to have so many people full or partially unproductive. We will do it because it is honest and fair for us to give all men and women their best chance in life."

The State Council was one of the chief forms of leadership for achieving this goal, the Governor said. He also announced that he was asking all mayors and chairmen of county commissions to establish local councils and that he was calling on church leaders, pastors, and civic organizations to support the objectives of the program. In addition, he reported that a memorandum had been sent to heads of State agencies, departments, and institutions asking them, if they had not already done so, to examine and formulate "policies which do not exclude from employment qualified people because of race."

For leadership of the entire Good Neighbor program and the chairmanship of the State Council, the Governor called upon David S. Coltrane, who was then serving as Special Consultant to the Governor on Economy and Efficiency. Coltrane is one of the most distinguished members of the government, commanding wide respect among both governmental and non-governmental groups across the State. Since entering government service in 1937, he has served as Assistant Commissioner and Commissioner of Agriculture, Assistant Director of the Budget, Director of the Department of Administration, chairman of the Advisory Budget Commission, and Special Consultant to the Governor. He has also held many prominent positions in agricultural, religious, academic and other groups outside the government.

Named to the vice chairmanship of the State Council by the Governor was Dr. James T. Taylor, a Negro leader who had been Dean of Men at North Carolina College until joining the State Employment Security Commission in 1963. As an Employment Counseling Supervisor at ESC, he has been responsible for encouraging private employers to hire on a merit basis and for encouraging young people to acquire a good education.

Announcement of the new program and its leadership drew a warm and enthusiastic response from the press. "All North Carolinians of good will wish for the Good Neighbor Councils every success in an endeavor which carries rich promise for a state and its people," said the

Charlotte *Observer.* In Raleigh, the *News and Observer* commented that "the entire economy of North Carolina and not merely its colored citizens would be served by Governor Sanford's Good Neighbor proposal . . ." The Greensboro *Daily News* agreed, observing that "a dollar-and-cents appeal coupled with the prodding of Tarheelia's deeply ingrained fairness and honesty, augurs well for the program behind which the Governor has thrown his leadership. His goal will not be obtained overnight, but, after all, it will be the long, steady, enduring pull, in the characteristic North Carolina way, which counts for most." The Sunday *Journal and Sentinel* in Winston-Salem told its readership that Coltrane "can be expected to be a fair-minded leader committed neither to trying to force desegregation on any employment nor to maintaining traditional patterns of discriminatory employment. Rather, he and his council can be expected to help employers see the advantage to their community and state in lifting the level of economic opportunity for a segment of the population whose lack of buying power holds back the entire state's economy." Similar views of the program were expressed by more than fifty other newspapers in the state and nation.

Amidst the flurry of press notices, Coltrane began to organize the Good Neighbor program on a state-wide basis. Within nine months, twenty of the State Council seats had been filled, a program had been drawn up for groups at the local and State level, leaders in thirteen areas had formed committees, and a number of employers had begun to hire on a merit basis. That initial thrust was highly important, for it gave the program a momentum and tone which have marked it ever since.

Today the State Council has 27 members in addition to Coltrane and Dr. Taylor. They come from all walks and include sixteen whites and eleven Negroes. At the first meeting of the group, Dr. John R. Larkins was elected Recording Secretary. Dr. Larkins is a special consultant on Negro affairs for the State Public Welfare Department and the author of several publications. His governmental position is one of the highest held by a Negro in the southeast.

Other members of the Council are Jeff D. Batts, Rocky Mount, attorney; Mrs. Geneva J. Bowe, Murfreesboro; Clark S. Brown, Winston-Salem, funeral director; Robert J. Brown, High Point, B & C Associates; Dr. G. K. Butterfield, Wilson, dentist; Mrs. Virginia Dameron, Asheville; Harry O. Gore, Southport; J. Marse Grant, Raleigh, editor of *The Biblical Recorder*; Thompson Greenwood, Raleigh, executive secretary of the North Carolina Merchants Association; Mrs. Geneva B. Hamilton, Goldsboro; Dr. Reginald A. Hawkins, Charlotte, dentist; J. W. Jeffries, Mebane, retired; John E. Jervis, West Asheville, Labor Union Representative; Bruce F. Jones, Edenton, automobile dealer; Edward Loewenstein, Greensboro, architect; J. A. Nelson, Charlotte, manager of administration at Douglas Aircraft; J. W. Pate, Jr., Fayetteville; Marshall A. Raugh, Gastonia, textile manufacturer; Ernest W. Ross, Albemarle, executive director of the Stanly County Industrial Committee; J. P. Strother, Kinston, associate editor of the Kinston *Free Press*; John H. Wheeler, Durham, president of Mechanics and Farmers Bank; John W. Winters, Raleigh, real estate broker and member of Raleigh City Council; and E. R. Zane, High Point, senior vice president of Burlington Industries, Inc.

Activities of the State Council

Nearly all activities of the State Council have been carried on or directed from the office of David S. Coltrane. He has generally conferred with the Governor before taking action on matters of a controversial nature. Advice and consent have also been sought on many occasions from the vice-chairman and the Council's executive committee, which is composed of members who live or work in Raleigh. Approximately once a quarter, the entire council has met to discuss the program and hear reports from local council leaders, employers, educators, and others.

Mrs. Sarah T. Herbin, left, employment service representative on the Council, interviews a job applicant.

The staff which Coltrane directs has been small, but active. In September, 1963, Governor Sanford announced that Mrs. Sarah Herbin of Greensboro had been appointed to work with the Council in cooperation with the Department of Administration and State Personnel Department. Her primary responsibility has been to recruit qualified Negroes for employment in State government, a field in which she previously acquired much experience as associate director of a merit employment program in the Southeastern Office of the American Friends Service Committee from 1957-1963. In addition to Mrs. Herbin, the Council has had the assistance of a young college graduate during the summers of 1963 and 1964 and the services of a full-time secretary. Funds for the entire staff have come from the State Government.

In its activities, the Council has relied upon the methods of persuasion, education, research and negotiation. It has no legal authority and has avoided high-pressure tactics. Following the lead of the Governor, it has appealed instead to the sense of fair play, good will, and economic interests of the people.

Since much of the water is uncharted, the Council's major activities have simply evolved as the leadership has become more acquainted with the problems and arrived at solutions. These activities can perhaps best be summarized under six headings, which follow below:

Assistance to local councils: As progress at the local level will ultimately determine whether the program is successful, the State Council's first interest has been to encourage the formation and activity of local councils across the State. Generally these councils have been organized after consultation with the State headquarters.

4

Joseph S. Grissom, personnel director, North Carolina Department of Revenue, consults with Mrs. Herbin.

Following the formation, Coltrane or a staff assistant has often visited an early meeting of the group to discuss the purpose of the program, the needs of the particular area, and the experiences which other communities have had. Thereafter, steady communication links have been maintained between the State office and the local group as the latter has reported periodically on its progress, while the office has pumped out information of general interest, reports on other communities, and suggestions for further activities.

The information of general interest sent from the State office has been heavy and diverse. In August, 1963, for instance, a 20-page booklet describing the program and containing eight suggestions for local action was prepared for all local council members. (The same booklet was sent by Governor Sanford to governors of all other states and has been distributed to numerous libraries.) At approximately the same time the State Council realized that local council members, school counselors and teachers, and many Negro youth were unfamiliar with the vocational training opportunities offered in North Carolina. By September, 1963, a 95-page booklet describing all major vocational programs was published and distributed to councils, high school counselors, libraries, and interested civic groups. As the supply of 1,300 copies was soon exhausted, a revised edition of the brochure was prepared this summer. During the summer months, the State office also supplied local councils and others with interpretations of the Civil Rights Act and the Economic Opportunity Act. The latter was summarized in an eight-page brief which pointed out the opportunities open to communities under the antipoverty bill and urged the councils to mobilize community forces as quickly as possible. Copies of all of this material are available upon request from the North Carolina Good Neighbor Council, Box 584, Raleigh, N. C.

Spreading the Message: In addition to its coordinating functions, the Council has tried to reach as many people as possible in face-to-face meetings. Numerous visits have been made to large private employers and civic groups to discuss the problems they face and to appeal for their assistance. Trips have also been made to schools and colleges, particularly the Negro schools, to talk with principals and teachers about their curriculums and to speak with students about new job opportunities and the responsibilities of citizenship. As of September 1, for purposes of illustration, Mrs. Herbin has personally spoken with 37 high school and college groups, six directors of technical institutes and industrial education centers, 12 college placement officers, 27 PTA, civic and church groups, and numerous consultants at nine regional meetings.

Concern with State Employment: A gradually expanding interest of the Council has been the employment practices of State governmental agencies. These agencies represent the greatest source of employment in the State, engaging some 41,000 North Carolinians on a regular basis. The agencies are not covered by the equal employment sections of the Civil Rights Act.

The Council, soon after its formation, sent memoranda to all agencies, calling their attention to the Governor's pledge for equal employment practices. In September, 1963, when Mrs. Herbin joined the Council, Governor Sanford wrote the agencies that "her appointment represents an effort to assure all citizens of North Carolina, white or Negro, that equal job opportunities exist in State employment. Of course we must insist upon qualified applicants and employees in the public interest of the State." Since that time, Mrs. Herbin and Coltrane have had many contacts with agency directors.

Mrs. Herbin, as of September 1, had interviewed approximately 400 Negro applicants for State jobs and had referred 225 of them to the State Personnel Office and/or to other agencies. Of this group, 31 placements had been made—24 in non-traditional positions with work in integrated facilities. The agencies and placements which accounted for this latter number were as follows: Prison Department, 10 prison guards and one dental technician; Department of Conservation and Development, one draftsman and one duplicating machine operator; Department of Revenue, one tax auditor; North Carolina Fund, one stenographer; North Carolina State College of the University of North Carolina at Raleigh, one stenographer; State Board of Health, two medical laboratory assistants; Department of Labor, one factory inspector; Purchase and Contract Division of the Department of Administration, one stock clerk; and the Department of Juvenile Correction, four male counselors.

To obtain a clearer picture of State employment, the Council during August conducted a survey of all agencies, determining precisely what positions Negroes held in the agencies and whether they were located in segregated facilities. Preliminary reports at press time indicated that with the exception of Negro colleges and institutions, the State agencies had limited Negro employment and most of the Negro employees were in semi-skilled, unskilled and service positions. As in previous contacts, the agencies cooperated fully with the Council's efforts. Many indicated they were seeking Negro employees but could not find qualified applicants. A full report on the survey was to be published in a short time.

Church and Press Relations: Warm support for the Good Neighbor program has been received from church leaders and from the press across the State. During 1963, information on the program was sent to more than 1,100 ministers. Further information is being supplied this year.

(Continued on page 16)

What Price Traffic Safety?

"Few are willing to pay the price. . . ."

The problem of traffic safety is a tartar. Like the cold war, it seems always with us. Things seem to be getting worse, with no assurance that they will get better. There are no easy answers, no panaceas. Safety programs come and go. Traffic laws are disregarded. Few view the present or the prospect with hope of improvement or concept of directions. The temptation is to look elsewhere for scapegoats, to reassure oneself that "it can't happen to me," and to point the finger while asserting "*I'm* a safe driver, but *he's* not."

"Few of us are willing to pay the price to reduce highway accidents," says Dr. John Morris.

"We have a very rough problem on our hands now because nothing seems to be working out for us from a mass persuasion standpoint. So what do we fall back on? We fall back on morality. We fall back on sloganeering. And we make very little dents with these. . . . There just aren't any magic formulae. . . ." says Dr. Harold Mendelsohn.

"Highway safety has been the biggest flop of my administration. . . . I think we've reached the point where there's complete disregard for highway safety and total disrespect for traffic laws," says Governor Terry Sanford.

Dr. *Henry B. Day, Jr., responds to class questions on equipment for testing drivers' vision. The Winston-Salem o p t o m e t r i s t took part in the AAMVA "Vision Testing" presentation at the Knapp Building.*

As if to punctuate their words, the crash of steel, glass, and chrome reverberates up and down our streets and highways, leaving a welter of human blood and a clutter of junk as reminders of lives put to waste. Eight, nine, and ten were killed in two-car head-on collisions on North Carolina roads within the space of a few weeks. The highway death toll reached almost 1,200 in the first nine months of 1964, virtually assuring an all-time high in road fatalities this year. The number of motor vehicles on the roads, road mileage, drivers and miles travelled all are at an all-time peak and still rising. (North Carolina has almost three times as many drivers and more than three times as many motor vehicles as twenty years ago. Specifically, the number of licensed drivers has increased from an estimated 900,000 in 1945 to 1,820,000 in 1955 to 2,343,000 in 1964. Motor vehicle registrations have risen from 684,000 in

North Carolina's Commissioner of Motor Vehicles and AAMVA president Edward Scheidt chats with driver license administrators prior to his luncheon address on "Traffic Safety."

1945 to 1,600,000 in 1955 to 2,220,000 in 1964. Projections indicate that both drivers and vehicles will total more than 2,400,000 next year.) The public attitude often ranges from an expressed opinion that the problem of traffic safety is insoluble to a notion that responsibility for safe driving involves only time spent behind the wheel. There is a widespread feeling that little can be done to help matters, so why bother.

Is this an accurate appraisal, a realistic approach, to our traffic safety problems? Actually, there are many continuing efforts to seek directions and to complement them with specific programs in safety research, driver education, safety engineering, driver licensing, vehicle inspection and enforcement. The first annual Southeastern Regional Safety Communication Seminar and the Annual Regional Training School for Driver License Personnel might be used to illustrate two segments of the many activities aimed at greater highway safety.

Dr. Mendelsohn made his above-quoted comments at the Safety Communication Seminar which was co-sponsored by the National Safety Council, the North Carolina Traffic Safety Council, and the Institute of Government in late July. Dr. Morris made his remarks to the Regional Driver License School which is sponsored by the American Association of Motor Vehicle Administrators and the Institute of Government in September. Both men, and their colleagues on the programs, are representative of a growing body of professional people who have begun to dedicate at least a portion of their time and energies to this problem. They work at different levels—national, state and local—in and out of government, but to the same over-all purpose. Dr. Mendelsohn, a social psychologist and a communication specialist at the University of Denver, was commissioned by the Naitonal Safety Council to study mass communications for safety and has come up with fresh ideas on changing basic attitudes through the mass media. For instance, his research indicates that the scare technique is relatively ineffective in promoting safe driving but that more affirmative approaches using situations and characters with which a driver can readily identify may have some effect. (This particular conclusion will undoubtedly dismay those who rely on the shock effect from publication of the latest accident tolls, place wrecked vehicles on court house lawns for all to see, and publish tracts like the archetype article "And Sudden Death.") Dr. Mendelsohn's colleague in this Safety Communication Seminar, Arch McKinlay, director of public information to the National Safety Council, agrees with Dr. Mendelsohn's findings and his convictions that "mass communication have to be looking into a sensible approach to help control traffic accidents."

Phil Ellis, director of the North Carolina Traffic Safety Council, has invoked Dr. Mendelsohn's principles in safety TV and radio spots for North Carolina.

Dr. Morris from Morehead City and Dr. Simmons Patrick from Kinston are co-chairmen of the advisory committee of the North Carolina Medical Society to the Department of Motor Vehicles. Through this committee a number of physicians throughout the state have made time available for advice on driver licensing and un-licensing. Drs. Patrick and Morris and their colleagues are concerned, among other things, with the problems of the older driver, with the epileptic, the diabetic, the alcoholic, the narcotic users, the suicidal, the mentally ill and the physically handicapped who want or have driver licenses. Their advice has medical weight in such matters as road testing and written testing. Similarly, optometrists are advising the Department of Motor Vehicles on matters relating to vision and vision testing. Dr. James N. Rowland of Oxford, a leader of the American Optometric Association in North Carolina introduced Dr. James H. Grout of Charlotte and Dr. Henry B. Day, Jr., of Winston-Salem to the AAMVA school for a day-long presentation on "Vision Testing." Dr. Grout had some ideas for strengthening driver licensing programs and driver performance. For example, he suggested the need for more frequent driving tests for myopic young drivers; demonstrated how a driver loses his

sense of speed at 70 miles per hour (perhaps explaining the number of one-car and rear end accidents on dual-lane turnpikes); and illustrated why special driving care is necessary at dawn and dusk ("your eyes are neither completely light-adjusted nor dark-adjusted").

Governor Sanford told his news conference that North Carolina's inability to reduce highway deaths has not come from poor planning. He said: "We had the best traffic programs with the least results . . . that's the test." In this connection North Carolina has cooperated with and participated in the programs of the President's Committee on Traffic Safety. Under the Governor's leadership a Coordinating Committee on Traffic Safety, composed of state agency heads, was set up to establish policy, and the North Carolina Traffic Safety Council, supported by funds from private donors, to organize citizens' support and safety programs throughout the state. For its part in enforcement of traffic laws, the North Carolina Highway Patrol has been singled out for each of the past eight years for the National Association of Chiefs of Police award as the outstanding such organization in the nation. Similar honors have been awarded the Driver License and the Driver Education and Accident Records divisions of the North Carolina Department of Motor Vehicles. Driver education programs in North Carolina have been recognized and the student school bus driver

Drs. Simmons Patrick and John Morris discuss medical problems in driver licensing at the AAMVA-Institute of Government Driver License School.

program praised. The written tests required for driver licenses in this state have been described as a model for other states to emulate. Driver and vision testing parts of the license requirements compare favorably with those in other states. Driver improvement clinics are a useful working part of the over-all plan. Financial responsibility is required by law of drivers. A state-wide automobile inspection program was tried for two years in the late forties, but since its repeal only spot checking for defects has been tried. The governor has raised again the question whether traffic cases should be removed from the criminal

(Continued on page 21)

HOW POPULATION AND ECONOMIC TRENDS MAY AFFECT WATER RESOURCES
in North Carolina

By Milton S. Heath, Jr., *Assistant Director, Institute of Government,* and
David Godschalk, *Planning Director, Gainesville, Florida*

Editor's Note: The authors have recently completed a study of water resource planning for the North Carolina Department of Water Resources which the Department intends to use as a foundation for its future planning. This article is based on a chapter of the Department's report growing out of the study: "Water Resource Planning in North Carolina."

A review of recent economic and population statistics for North Carolina shows several notable trends. The State has had a consistent record of over-all population growth in this century, but owing to a high rate of out-migration North Carolina grew only two-thirds as fast as the nation in the 1950's. The State's over-all record of growth in the last decade was not evenly distributed, because there has been a ferment of movement from farm to city as well as out-migration. Consequently, the over-all 1950's growth breaks down into a declining rural farm population (down more than 40%), and a rising urban population (up over 30%) and rural nonfarm population (up over 40%).

Other trends include relative gains in white collar employment compared to blue collar employment; an increasing diversification of manufacturing; and growing automation of capital intensive industries with an incidental decrease in the workweek and increase in leisure time.

Growth and change in the State's population and economy have obvious significance for the use and management of water resources. Thus, it may be useful to scan the trends for clues as to their impact on future water demand, which is a function of consumer demand by people and economic demand for products whose production requires water.

People and Water

Population Growth

People use water in a variety of ways ranging from direct consumption and use for sanitary purposes to such indirect uses as recreation and esthetic enjoyment. A simple ratio of projected state population growth times estimated municipal per capita consumption indicates the following future needs:

NORTH CAROLINA MUNICIPAL WATER USE TRENDS

	1954	1980	2000
Urban Population (millions)	1.6	2.9	4.8
Per Capita Use (gallons per day—gpd)	108	106	106
Total Urban Use (million gallons per day—mgd)	169	312	507

These figures, published in Committee Print No. 7 of the Select Committee on National Water Resources, U. S. Senate, reflect their medium range population projections, and are broken down into the following amounts of average daily per capita use: 41% domestic, 18% commercial, 24% industrial, and 17% public. The estimated figure for North Carolina's future per capita use is probably conservative. The State Board of Health currently estimates the average municipal consumption in major urban areas as between 100 and 125 gallons per person per day, as compared with a national average of 147 gallons per person per day. Although this has apparently leveled off, future technological innovations could cause a significant change. The averages can be misleading, too, for various segments of the State. For example, a recent planning report covering the heart of the Piedmont assumes a considerably larger and rising per capita

use for this area.[1]

Population Movements

Population movement from farms to cities will increasingly localize demand in the highly urbanized areas. The North Carolina Division of Community Planning has estimated that about two-thirds of the 1980 population will be located in the Piedmont region. A trend to an increasing rural non-farm population is notable in recent census figures. These population movements are likely to be significant for water resource use and development in several ways.

• The probable concentration of population in Piedmont cities will impose major stresses on water supply and waste disposal and treatment facilities of the urban areas. North Carolina's larger cities have a generally good record of planning for water supplies. Moreover the overall record of the State as to waste treatment facilities is quite good, owing largely to an unusually vigorous State water pollution abatement program. Thus we are currently in good position to meet these coming stresses, but this should be no cause for complacency; heavy additional expenditures for water supply and waste disposal will be needed in the impacted urban areas.

• A companion effect of these population trends will be to increase required minimum stream flows for waste dilution, necessitating larger investments for flow regulation as well as pollution abatement measures. This conclusion is reinforced by the expressions of leading observors concerning the intense importance of waste dilution requirements in future water resource programs in the southeastern United States. For example, the Senate Select Committee on Na-

1. "Report on Seven Cities Water Project, Yadkin River," Piatt and Davis, Wm. C. Olsen and Assoc., Hazen and Sawyer, Engineers, 1957.

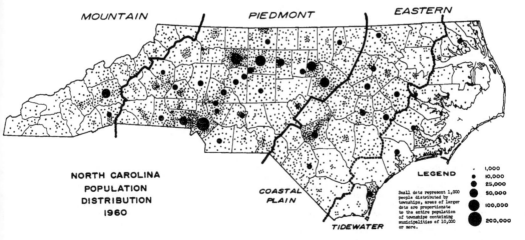

MOUNTAIN   PIEDMONT   EASTERN

NORTH CAROLINA
POPULATION
DISTRIBUTION
1960

COASTAL
PLAIN

TIDEWATER

LEGEND
. 1,000
● 10,000
● 25,000
● 50,000
● 100,000
● 200,000

Small dots represent 1,000
people distributed by
townships, areas of larger
dots are proportionate
to the entire population
of townships containing
municipalities of 10,000
or more.

Source: U. S. CENSUS BUREAU

tional Water Resources in its final report (Committee Print #32) estimates that the southeast with its average annual rainfall of 51 inches, average stream flows of 207 b.g.d. and minimum flows of 21 b.g.d. should be able to readily meet projected needs for water use to the year 2000 — *if* stream flows are adequately regulated by storage[2]. It should therefore be a prime objective of water resource planning in North Carolina to encourage the development of the needed storage facilities and the operation of these facilities to achieve optimum flow augmentation benefits.

• The population movements will also impose new strains upon water rights laws by causing an increase in the incidence and intensity of water use conflicts. These and other developments — such as the growing demand for water recreation and the potential expansion of farm irrigation — are likely to hasten the day when the existing legal structure for water rights will require thoughtful reexamination.

• The trend toward an increasing rural non-farm population may have

2. See also Tolley, G. S. and Riggs, F. E., *Water Allocation In a Resource-Oriented Subregion.* Southeastern Water Law Conference, proceedings: "Water Law and Policy in the Southeast." Athens, Georgia (1961).

several causes — notably, the movement of farm dwellers into non-farm occupations and the known preference of many new industrial plants for locations outside the cities. This trend, if continued, will pose difficult problems for public water supply and waste disposal which should be anticipated by state agencies working in cooperation with local governments.

Outdoor Recreation

Yet another expectation is increased demand for water-based outdoor recreational resources. Demand for recreation of all types has expanded at an unparalleled rated in recent years, and the Outdoor Recreation Resources Review Commission, reporting to the President and Congress in 1962, stated, "Not only will there be more people, they will want to do more, and they will have more money and time to do it with. By the year 2000 the Nation's population is expected to double; the demand for recreation should be triple." The reduction in work weeks and increases in leisure, coupled with an expected rise in personal incomes, will spur the growth of recreation demand, much of which will be for boating, fishing, swimming, skiing, and other types of water recreation. North Carolina's resources and programs for public recreation already show significant gaps; efforts to improve them, therefore,

certainly appear to deserve a high priority.

Water and the Economy

The Senate Select Committee on Water Resources has concluded that water appears to be the limiting factor in population and general economic growth in five western regions. The eastern regions, including North Carolina, are less limited, and their major problem is to provide an adequate supply for waste dilution.

The heaviest commitments of the North Carolina economy are now in agriculture and manufacturing. In agriculture water is needed principally for supplemental irrigation of crops. Manufacturing depends on water as an integral part of its production processes, for disposal of process waste, and as a coolant.

Agriculture

Presumably as more people leave the farms for urban life the agriculture process will be characterized by larger land holdings and more mechanization. Through this process of consolidation the state will be enabled to take a larger part in the "agricultural revolution" which has raised agricultural productivity in other parts of the nation. One of the results involving water resources may be a further increase in irrigation.

Agricultural irrigation is larvely a postwar phenomenon in North Carolina. Since soils and terrain are suited to sprinkling rather than ditch-type irrigation, the increased use has resulted from the development of inexpensive, lightweight aluminum and plastic piping. Due to the capital investment required for an irrigation system, even with aluminum piping, most users are producers of crops yielding a high return per acre such as tobacco, flowers, nursery items, and small fruit or truck crops. Primary water sources are streams in the Mountain region, ponds in the Piedmont, and ground water in the Eastern region[3].

There has been a continuous record of growth in irrigated acreage in North Carolina for more than a decade — from a nominal acreage before 1950 to more than 70,000 acres· today according to estimates by irrigation experts. Several factors will influence the future growth rate of irrigation. One of these will doubtless be the rate of consolidation of farm land holdings, mentioned above. Also quite important is the future of the tobacco industry both nationally and in this State, for tobacco has been by far the principal irrigated crop in the State. Not only does it account for most of the total irrigated acreage but in many cases farmers irrigating other crops do so only incidentally, after having acquired irrigation equipment for their tobacco.

The future of tobacco farming is significant in terms of location as well as to quantity of water use. For example, studies have shown that flue-cured tcbacco can be grown much more efficiently in the Coastal Plain than in the Piedmont region. If the present tobacco allotment system were revised to permit allotments to be freely transferable on a state-wide basis, there would be substantial incentives for moving Piedmont tobacco holdings to the East. In terms of overall water supply and demand this could minimize the likelihood of conflicts between agricultural water usage and industrial and domestic usage in the urbanizing Piedmont unless other profitable applications for irrigation were meanwhile developed. A reduction of such conflicts would in turn relieve pressures that might otherwise develop for water rights law revision.

Obviously, future developments in farm irrigation are an important element in the overall water economy and should be monitored closely by water resource planners.

Industry

North Carolina's "big three" industries in terms of employment and payrolls are textiles, tobacco, and furniture. Other significant manufacturing segments include apparel, food processing, electrical and other machinery, chemicals, pulp and paper, and lumber.

Some of these industries have unusually large water requirements for process, cooling and waste dilution. This group would include food processing, textiles, chemicals and pulp and paper. The others do not ordinarily pose major problems for water supply. (These are of course broad generalizations which cover a wide range of needs and practices within each industrial grouping.)

Recent growth trends in these industrial groups show significant expansion in furniture, apparel and machinery (minor water users), and in food processing (a major water user); slight expansion in pulp and paper and in chemicals (major water users); and declining significance for textiles (a major water user), as well as for tobacco and lumber (minor water users). The implications fo· water resource development, assuming a continuance of these trends, offer a mixed picture which defies generalizations.

In a survey of new industrial plants by Mrs. Ruth Mace it has been found that new plant locations are rarely affected by the availability of public water or sewer facilities, except in the heavy water using industries. New industries often tend to take for granted the availability of such facilities — sometimes to their later regret[4].

Industrial growth stimulates a growth in demand for electric power which is also closely related to water use. Generally power production is handled today with a combination of hydro-electric generators for peak loads, and steam-electric generators for base loads. The hydro-electric installations function directly on water

flows, while steam-electric plants use very large quantities of water for cooling. Nationwide, cooling water for steam-electric utilities is the largest non-agricultural withdrawal use. Expansion plans of North Carolina's principal electric energy suppliers foreshadow an increasing reliance upon steam generation for new installations in the next ten to twenty years, which will correspondingly enlarge their needs for cooling water. The effects upon water supplies will be a subject of increasing interest for water resource agencies.

Conclusion

The highlights of this review of economic conditions and their impact upon water resource development can be briefly summarized.

Economic and population trends point to increasing demands upon water resources in a number of areas, notably for dilution of industrial wastes and domestic sewage, for water-based recreation, for cooling purposes in steam-electric generating plants, and for public water supplies. Farm irrigation requirements have been growing rapidly and will probably continue to grow, but the rate and incidence of this growth are difficult to prophecy.

The more compelling needs likely to follow will include development and operation of increased storage reservoirs to impound streams and regulate their flows, and a considerable expansion in public water recreation facilities and programs. There may also be resulting pressures for revision of water rights laws, and there will certainly be a need for greatly expanded water resource planning and research programs.

Finally, the impact of economic trends upon water resources will probably be rather selective. Some areas have already tasted impending problems brought on by expanded economies — for example, the Seven Cities Region of the central Piedmont, in terms of water supply and conflicts between recreation and power generation; the Roanoke River Basin, in terms of a complex water quality problem embracing reservoir operations, paper mill wastes and fishery resources; and the Research Triangle Region, in terms of a mixture of water supply, waste disposal and water recreation needs. However, some other parts of the State have encountered

3. Heath, Milton S., Jr. and Martin, James E., Jr., *Survey of Irrigation in Selected North Carolina Counties 1962.* Paper No. 2, U.N.C. Water Resource Papers. Institute of Government, University of North Carolina, Chapel Hill (1962).

4. Mace, Ruth L., *Industry and City Government.* Institute of Government, University of North Carolina, Chapel Hill (1963).

(Continued inside back cover)

Commitment to Jail:

A SUMMARY OF NORTH CAROLINA LAW AND PROCEDURE

By James C. Harper, *Research Assistant,*
Institute of Government

North Carolina county jail records reveal that the majority of persons confined at any given time are awaiting trial on a criminal charge. Others incarcerated include (1) those serving sentence imposed upon conviction for a misdemeanor; (2) those awaiting transfer to the State's prison after conviction for a felony or after having been sentenced to work under the prison system following conviction for a misdemeanor; (3) those awaiting the outcome of an appeal from a conviction; (4) federal prisoners serving sentence or awaiting trial or transfer to a federal prison;[1] (5) persons committed to jail for contempt of court; (6) persons temporarily detained in jail pending a hearing of one sort or another in a matter involving mental illness or inebriacy, or awaiting transportation to a state institution for the mentally ill or inebriate;[2] (7) juvenile offenders awaiting transportation to an appropriate institution,[3] or (8) debtors confined under an order of civil arrest or execution against the person.[4]

Almost as varied as the types of prisoners confined in the county jails are the procedures and laws under which they are committed, though there exists a more or less standard rule which must be followed before any person may be lawfully confined in jail for any reason. To paraphrase a portion of the Fourteenth Amendment to the Constitution of the United States, that rule is simply that no person may be deprived of his liberty but through due process of law. If a man is put in jail, he is deprived of his liberty in a very real sense; thus, it

shall be our object here to pick out and discuss the due process of law under which a man's liberty may be taken away in this fashion.

It is required by a very old statute in this State that "No person shall be imprisoned by any judge, court, justice of the peace, or other peace officer except in the common jail of the county, unless otherwise provided by law."[5] It is otherwise provided by law that persons convicted of criminal offenses may be imprisoned in the State's prison or prison camps; that certain types of offenders may be committed to correctional and training institutions, and, at least by implication, that persons may be committed to municipal jails and lock-ups to await trail or serve sentence imposed after conviction.

Another North Carolina statute provides that commitment before conviction must in all cases be to the jail of the county where the preliminary examination is had or in which the offense is alleged to have been committed.[6] Literally construed, this section would require that all persons arrested and charged with crime (where bail is not set or cannot be met) be confined in the county jail. Such an interpretation would preclude commitment of such persons to municipal jails; thus, it is necessary to conclude that more recent statutory authority for municipal jails impliedly authorizes commitment of persons awaiting trial to municipal jails.[7]

If for any reason there is no jail in a county, the sheriff and other officers of such county are authorized to commit prisoners to jail in any other adjoining county. Similarly, if a county has a jail that is found to be unfit or insecure, magistrates and judges are authorized to commit or sentence prisoners to the jail of an adjoining county, and the jailer of the adjoining county is obliged to honor such commitment or be guilty of a misdemeanor. And when any county

jail is destroyed by fire or other casualty, there is authority for transfer of prisoners to another jail. By and large, there is little reason to belabor the discussion of *where* persons charged with or convicted of crime may be imprisoned; a more important body of law and procedure lies in methods by which such persons may be lawfully committed.

The principal statute[8] prescribing procedures for commitment of persons *charged with crime* provides:

Every commitment to prison of a person charged with crime shall state:

1. The name of the person charged.
2. The character of the offense with which he is charged.
3. The name and office of the magistrate commiting him.
4. The manner in which he may be discharged; if upon giving recognizance or bail, the amount of the recognizance, the condition on the performance of which it shall be discharged, and the persons or magistrate before whom the bail may justify.
5. The court before which the prisoner shall be sent for trial.

It may be readily seen that if this statute were strictly followed, no person could ever be committed to jail by an arresting officer prior to the issuance of a commitment order by a magistrate. But this is not the case; for if it were, many jailers would often be guilty of a misdemeanor if they followed the letter of the statute quoted above.[9] Moreover, there is other express authority for commitment of persons to jail by arresting officers. A statute[10] enacted the same year and in the same bill as the one quoted above provides:

Every person arrested without warrant shall be either immediately taken before some magis-

1. See N.C. Gen. Stat. § 153-183 (1964).
2. In connection with commitment to institutions of inebriate or mentally ill persons, interim confinement in the jail is a rare occurrence, though required at times as an emergency measure. See N.C. Gen. Stat. Ch. 122, arts. 6, 7 (1964).
3. There are strict requirements concerning the confinement of juvenile offenders in the county jail. See N.C. Gen. Stat. Ch. 110, art. 2 (1960).
4. See Harper, *North Carolina Sheriffs' Manual,* Institute of Government (1964). Ch. IV.

5. N.C. Gen. Stat. § 15-6 (1953).
6. N.C. Gen. Stat. § 15-126 (1953).
7. See N.C. Gen. Stat. § 160-2(10) (1964).

8. N.C. Gen. Stat. § 15-125 (1953).
9. N.C. Gen. Stat. § 153-190.1 (1964).
10. N.C. Gen. Stat. § 15-46 (1953).

trate having jurisdiction to issue a warrant in the case, or else committed to the county prison, and, as soon as may be, taken before such magistrate, who, on proper proof, shall issue a warrant and thereon proceed to act as may be required by law.

In view of the fact that both the preceding statutes were enacted in the same chapter, it is apparent that "thereon proceed to act as may be required by law" in the latter statute refers to the former, thus requiring that the committing magistrate issue a commitment order in conformity with the former section at the time he issues a warrant for a person who has been arrested and temporarily committed to jail by the arresting officer.

The duties of the arresting officer with respect to arrest and detention of a person charged with a crime are spelled out in a more recent enactment:[11]

Upon the arrest, detention, or deprivation of the liberties of any person by an officer in this State, with or without warrant, it shall be the duty of the officer making the arrest to immediately inform the person arrested of the charge against him, and it shall further be the duty of the officer making said arrest, except in capital cases, to have bail fixed in a reasonable sum, and the person so arrested shall be permitted to give bail bond; and it shall be the duty of the officer making the arrest to permit the person so arrested to communicate with counsel and friends immediately, and the right of such persons to communicate with counsel and friends shall not be denied. Provided that in no event shall the prisoner be kept in custody for a longer period than twelve hours without a warrant. . . .

Thus, read together with the other two statutes set out above, this section sets an outside limit upon the time in which an arresting officer must obtain a warrant after arresting and committing a person without one. That limit is twelve hours. Furthermore, if all three statutes are met with compliance, both by the arresting officer and the magistrate before whom such officer appears to obtain a warrant, at the time he issues the warrant

11. N.C. Gen. Stat. § 15-47 (Supp. 1963). [Emphasis added.]

12

of arrest the magistrate must also issue a commitment order. Since one requisite of a valid commitment order is a provision fixing bail, it seems that the officer's duty to have bail fixed in a reasonable sum would be met in most cases when the commitment order issues.

In addition to the statutes quoted above, the North Carolina Supreme Court has handed down an opinion in point. In State v. Freeman,[12] a man was placed in jail by a constable after having been found helplessly drunk on a public sidewalk. The next morning the mayor of the town issued a warrant for the arrest of that person, who was then taken before the mayor for trial. He was found guilty of violating a town ordinance proscribing public drunkenness. Promptly thereafter, the defendant brought a criminal charge against the constable for false imprisonment, alleging that he had been unlawfully confined in jail by the constable at a time when the mayor of the town was available for an immediate hearing on the charge against him. The constable appealed from his conviction. In reversing the conviction of assault and false imprisonment, the Court said:

Holding that a person may be arrested for drunkenness upon view, when it is a public nuisance, the question occurs, what is the officer to do with the offender when he shall have been arrested without warrant? All the authorities agree that he should be carried, as soon as conveniently may be, before some justice of the peace. And if he is arrested at a time and under such circumstances as he cannot be carried immediately before a justice of the peace, the officer may keep him in custody, commit him to jail or the lock-up, or even tie him, according to the nature of the offense and the necessity of the case. . . .[13]

Before the twelve-hour limitation was added to G.S. 15-47,[14] the North Carolina Supreme Court had occasion to review a case[15] where the defendant convicted of murder asserted that his arrest and commitment to jail without warrant was in violation of the then G.S. 15-47. In that case the defendant was arrested without war-

12. 86 N.C. 683 (1882).
13. Ibid. p. 686. See also Perry v. Hurdle, 229 N.C. 216, 49 S.E.2d 400 (1948).
14. Session Laws 1955, Ch. 889.
15. State v. Exum, 213 N.C. 16, 195 S.E. 7 (1938).

rant and confined in a jail in another county for what appears to have been several days before a warrant charging him with murder was obtained. In holding that the arrest and commitment were not in violation of the statute (and consequently that the confession of the defendant during the period of his confinement and before the warrant issued was admissible), the Court said:

The evidence at the trial shows that immediately after his arrest, the defendant was informed by the sheriff that he was charged with . . . murder. . . . This is a capital case. For this reason the provisions of the statute with respect to bail are not applicable. . . .

There is no evidence in the record tending to show that after his arrest and while he was in custody of the sheriff the defendant demanded of the sheriff that he be permitted to communicate with friends or with counsel. For this reason the provisions of the statute with respect to the right of a defendant in the custody of an officer and charged with the commission of a crime, to communicate with friends and counsel are not applicable. . . .[16]

But since counsel for the defendant apparently did not assert that the sheriff had violated G.S. 15-46, the Court said nothing about the fact that the defendant was held in jail for several days before he was taken before a magistrate as required by that section. Nor did the Court say anything about the fact that the defendant was committed to a jail in another county. Had these issues been raised by the defendant, it appears that in light of prior decisions of the Court on the reasonableness of the time factor between the arrest and commitment of the defendant and the issuance of a warrant,[17] the several days that apparently elapsed between the defendant's arrest and the issuance of a warrant may have been unreasonable. This then leads to a question of who may be liable under the present state of the law if a defendant is arrested without warrant and kept in jail more than twelve hours before a warrant is procured.

16. Id. 213 N.C. at 22.
17. See State v. Freeman, 86 N.C. 683 (1882); Hobbs v. Washington, 168 N.C. 293, 84 S.E. 391 (1915); Perry v. Hurdle, 229 N.C. 216, 49 S.E.2d 400 (1948).

There is no punitive provision in G.S. 15-46; however, in *Hobbs v. Washington*,[18] the Court held that the officer who arrested the defendant without warrant, and then failed to comply with the requirement to take him before a magistrate, was personally answerable in damages. But any person who falsely arrests or imprisons another may be sued for damages. As to *criminal* liability on the part of jailers and arresting officers, it is declared to be a misdemeanor for the former to refuse to accept prisoners delivered to their jails under certain circumstances.[19] It is also a misdemeanor for an arresting officer to fail to do a number of things upon an arrest, one of which is to obtain a warrant within twelve hours after arresting a person and holding him in custody without a warrant.[20] However, except where a prisoner is delivered by a municipal officer of a municipality having its own jail, or by an officer who arrested the prisoner outside the county where commitment is sought, the jailer has no authority to question the officer who delivers a prisoner for detention in the jail, whether the arrest was with or without warrant or whether or not a commitment order has been issued. As to the liability of a jailer where a prisoner is held in jail longer than twelve hours without a warrant having been issued, Professor Watts has said:

It is my belief that despite G.S. 153-190.1 the jailer as well as the arresting officer may become liable if a person is held in jail without warrant longer than twelve hours to the knowledge of the jailer. The arresting officer is liable, of course, if he has a man held in jail *any* length of time when a magistrate is in fact available, for the law commands him to take the prisoner to the magistrate immediately; twelve hours is just the outside limit. Under the policy lying behind G.S. 153-190.1, though, the jailer would probably not share in the guilt of the arresting officer in such a situation where less than twelve hours passes unless the jailer *actively* encourages the arresting officer in the violation of the prisoner's constitutional rights.

To the extent that G.S. 153-

190.1 could be considered as excusing a county jailer from participating in an affirmative and knowing denial of the constitutional rights of a prisoner, I believe it would be held invalid by the courts.[21]

There being no reason to doubt the correctness of Professor Watts' conclusion, then, it appears that so long as a jailer does not wilfully and knowingly aid and abet an arresting officer in depriving a person of his constitutional rights by keeping him in jail without proper process having been obtained, the jailer would not be liable, either civilly or criminally, for any wrongful acts or omissions on the part of the arresting officer.

In concluding the discussion of commitment of persons charged with crime, while there may be a number of questions left unanswered, it appears that (1) except in cases expressly excluded by G.S. 153-190.1, it is the duty of every county jailer in North Carolina to accept all prisoners delivered by arresting officers; (2) in case of arrest without warrant, it is the duty of the arresting officer to obtain a warrant as soon as possible within twelve hours; (3) in case of arrest with or without warrant, it is the duty of the arresting officer to immediately or as quickly as possible take the accused person before a magistrate; (4) in a case where the accused person is taken before a magistrate before he is delivered to the jail, a written commitment order should accompany his commitment, and (5) in a case where the accused person is delivered to the jail before being taken before a magistrate, when and if he is returned to the jail, he should be accompanied by a written commitment order.

In between, so to speak, persons committed to jail awaiting trial or hearing and those committed after being sentenced by a court to imprisonment, are probation violators who, though free under the conditions of suspension of sentence, may be re-arrested and re-committed to jail. In this regard, a single reference to a statute is deemed to be sufficient:

At any time during the period of probation or suspension of sentence, the court may issue a warrant and cause the defendant to be arrested for violating any

of the conditions of probation or suspension of sentence. Any police officer, or other officer with power of arrest, upon the request of the probation officer, may arrest a probationer without a warrant. In case of an arrest without a warrant the arresting officer shall have a written statement signed by said probation officer setting forth that the probationer has, in his judgment, violated the conditions of probation; and said statement shall be sufficient warrant for the detention of said probationer in the county jail, or other appropriate place of detention, until said probationer shall be brought before the judge of the court. . . .[22]

Thus, under the foregoing authority, the arresting officer may deliver a probationer, along with a written statement signed by the probation officer and setting forth that in the opinion of the probation officer the probationer has violated the terms of his probation, to the jail where he must be kept until further order from the appropriate court.

With respect to temporary detention in the county jail of persons enroute to other institutions — namely, the State prison system — there are some specific statutory provisions which ought to be mentioned. The first of these provisions[23] pertains to the duties of the county sheriff with respect to interim custody and transportation. It provides that when a person convicted of a felony is sentenced to central prison, a sheriff or other appropriate officer of the county shall cause such prisoner to be delivered with the proper commitment papers to the warden of the central prison.

Another statute[24] provides that the sheriff having charge of a prisoner sentenced to central prison must send him to the prison within five days after adjournment of the court at which he was sentenced, if no appeal has been taken. The latter provision also provides that the State is not liable for expenses in maintaining any prisoner until he has been received by the State Prison Department authorities, and that "the sheriff shall file with the board of county commissioners of his county a copy of his itemized

(Continued on page 18)

18. 168 N.C. 293, 84 S.E. 391 (1915).
19. N.C. Gen. Stat. § 153-190.1 (1964).
20. N.C. Gen. Stat. § 15-47 (Supp. 1963).

21. Letter from L. Poindexter Watts, Assistant Director, Institute of Government, to North Carolina Law Enforcement Officers, July 27, 1963.

22. N.C. Gen. Stat. § 15-200 (Supp. 1963).
23. N.C. Gen. Stat. § 148-28 (1964).
24. N.C. Gen. Stat. § 148-29 (1964).

INSTITUTE SCHOOLS, MEETINGS, CONFERENCES

Pictured above are members of the Uniform Costs and Fees Committee of the Association of Clerks of Superior Court, meeting at the Institute of Government in October. From left to right are Russell Nipper, Wake County Clerk; C. E. Hinsdale, assistant director, Institute of Government; D. M. McLelland, Alamance County Clerk; Ben Neville, Nash County Clerk; and Taylor McMillan, Assistant Director, Institute of Government. Object of the session was to recommeind a uniform court costs and fees bill to the Courts Commission, at the request of the Commission.

In cooperation with the University of North Carolina School of Library Science and the North Carolina State Library, the Institute held a three-day workshop on state and local documents as library resources. Pictured above left is Institute Librarian Olga Palotai speaking to some of the 40 conferees. In the classroom scene above right, Miss Sangster Parrott, State Library Technical Services librarian, is seated at lower right.

Shown below are driver license examiners who attended a school at the Institute of Government in October. Assistant Director Robert L. Gunn had charge of the in-service school which is held annually for all license examiners.

Institute Assistant Director Robert Stipe teaches a graduate level course on planning legislation in the UNC Department of City and Regional Planning. The class, above, will consider such topics as enabling legislation for planning, urban and rural zoning, subdivision and other land use controls, urban redevelopment law, aind housng legislation.

Pictured on the opposite page, right, is a class session in a five-day school for new tax supervisors conducted in the Knapp Building by Institute of Government Assistant Director Henry W. Lewis. The school is offered annually.

Beginning in October the Institute of Government launched its first annual course in police administration. The nine-week program is designed to provide supervisory personnel with a proper foundation in the management of police operations. Characterized by an integrated, multidisciplinary approach, the course includes lectures, assigned readings, written reports, individual and group projects, and class discussions. Some of the participants in the program are pictured at top, center, and below left. Shown above right is George Eastman, Chicago public administration expert, lecturing on police administration.

Professor Frank Day, above, police science instructor at Michigan State University, lectures on "Crime and the Youthful Offender," during one of the Police Administration Course sessions. Among numerous other areas covered in the course are police history, constitutional law, sociology, communication, public and press relationship, traffic engineering, and crowd and mob behavior.

The Good Neighbor Council

(Continued from page 5)

The Council has also made a special effort to disseminate the views of the press on race relations and the Good Neighbor program.

Center of Intelligence: As the material above would suggest, one of the Council's main functions has been to act as a State communications center on many racial matters. The Council has been in regular contact with many individuals and groups within the State, and with organizations outside the State such as the West Virginia Human Rights Commission, the Southern Regional Council, and the recently-formed Community Relations Service of the Federal government.

Trouble-Shooting: Governor Sanford has asked General Gapus Waynick to represent his office in most of the racial disputes which have arisen in the last sixteen months. In several instances, however, Coltrane has stepped in to obtain a full report for the Governor or to assist in keeping the peace. One of the most recent occasions came this summer when the Ku Klux Klan threatened to break-up a church-painting by an integrated group visiting Elm City. Coltrane visited the area to help reduce the possibility of violence and to establish firm communication lines between Raleigh and Elm City.

Efforts at the Local Level

At the local level, Good Neighbor councils or bi-racial committees have generally been organized by the mayor or other high-ranking officials of a community. In some instances, interested individuals or groups have been instrumental in spurring the formation. A few bi-racial committees existed before January, 1963, but most of them have been formed since that date. At press time, councils or human relations groups concerned with education and employment had been named in the following 47 communities: Alamance County, Albemarle, Asheboro, Asheville, Brevard, Chapel Hill, Charlotte, Clinton, Dunn, Durham, Edenton, Elizabeth City, Fayetteville, Gastonia, Goldsboro, Greensboro, Greenville, Hickory, High Point, Kinston, Laurinburg, Lenoir, Lexington, Mooresville, Mount Airy, Murfreesboro, Newport, Oxford, Raleigh, Rockingham, Roxboro, Rocky Mount, Salisbury, Sanford, Shelby, Smithfield, Southern Pines, Tarboro, Thomasville, Wadesboro, Warrenton, Washington, Whiteville, Williamston, Wilmington, Wilson, and Winston-Salem.

Activities of the councils have often followed a similar pattern. In their early meetings, the groups have tried to acquaint themselves with the status of the local Negro, immediate job prospects for all citizens, future manpower needs, and the available training sources. Visits have then been made to employers to discuss their employment practices and appeal for their cooperation. Following these calls, the councils have tried to inform the Negro community of job possibilities and to impress upon them the urgent need for training. The councils in some cases have also recruited qualified Negroes on a small scale, promoted training programs, and sponsored workshops in which students, teachers, and guidance counselors have met with the major employers of the community to discuss job opportunities.

The dedication and success of the councils has of course varied from area to area. Although most of the councils have been active, some have lagged badly. An account of the more notable community activities and

signs of progress follows below:

Charlotte. Through the efforts of the mayor, the Community Relations Service which he formed, the Chamber of Commerce, and certain professional and labor organizations, Charlotte has become a Southern leader in race relations. Mayor Stan R. Brookshire is chairman of the North Carolina Mayors' Co-operation Committee, a group which has worked closely with the Governor and local communities in preserving peace and open lines of communication. At a recent meeting of the State Good Neighbor Council, the Mayor explained that "Between the obvious alternatives, we in Charlotte have chosen to adjust the inequities imposed upon some of our citizens by patterns of the past and to pursue a policy of nondiscrimination in order to insure equal rights, opportunities and motivation for all of our citizens. . . . Much has been accomplished, and much still remains to be done. The important thing is that through earnest effort, cooperation, and patience we are making progress."

The Community Relations Service subcommittee on economic opportunities has devoted most of its time to encouraging merit practices in hiring and upgrading. In May, the full Committee sponsored a symposium on merit employment for the Charlotte business community. Representatives from several local companies were included among the speakers.

Progress in the employment of Negroes in non-traditional jobs has been noted in several areas, including the county and municipal governments, utility companies, department stores, banks, grocery stores, and an airline. From the encouragement of various groups in the area, one company which previously hired all whites in its northern location has employed on a merit basis since it relocated in Charlotte.

Greensboro: The Commission on Human Relations, and more particularly its Committee on Education and Job Opportunity, have spearheaded a strong effort to open new job opportunities and prepare students in the Greensboro area. With the assistance of the Retail Merchants Association, the Committee has had a full-time representative to coordinate its program. The work of all of these groups is thought to have been a major factor in the Labor Department's selection of Greensboro as the site for a pilot program which will train minority groups for employment.

The American Friends Service Committee, the YMCA, and the YWCA have also been active in the area. In May, with the aid of the Human Relations Committee, they sponsored a job clinic for all youth of the Greensboro area. This fall a special "brush-up" extension course for Negro girls who have received some secretarial training has been instituted at A&T College under the leadership of Dr. Lewis C. Dowdy, Mrs. Herbin, and the AFSC.

Latest reports on employment indicate that 50 percent of all non-agricultural jobs in Greensboro are controlled by employers who are now hiring on a merit basis. Employment of Negroes has been noted in several industries, banks, and retail stores.

Winston-Salem: Since World War II, Winston-Salem has been at the forefront of North Carolina communities trying to obtain equal opportunities for all citizens. Substantive progress has often come slowly, but as a result of efforts over a period of years, Negroes in Forsyth County today have a higher income than Negroes in any other county in the State. The county as a whole stands second only to Mecklenburg in family income.

16

POPULAR GOVERNMENT

North Carolina Good Neighbor Council Chairman D. S. Coltrane answers a telephone inquiry. He also serves as special consultant to the Governor on Economy and Efficiency in Government.

In 1963, a permanent bi-racial committee was appointed by the mayor to work in the areas of public accommodations, education, and employment. The group found that in the city government, Negroes hold nearly 700 of the 1700 jobs and are employed as clerks, stenographers, switchboard operators, nurses, pharmacists, laboratory technicians, librarians, fire sergeants, police patrolmen and detectives. Eighteen industries and businesses surveyed by the committee also indicated that they now employ Negroes in positions above the unskilled level. At latest report, the bi-racial committee wished to meet with industrial representatives to consider means of improving employment opportunities.

Goldsboro: The zeal and imagination of several individuals have turned Goldsboro into a center of progress in eastern North Carolina. The employment committee of the city's bi-racial council discovered a year ago that many jobs were opening up, but few Negroes were trained. With the assistance of various organizations, including the industrial education center, the Employment Security Commission, the city newspaper, and radio stations, some thirty-two people were given aptitude tests and were encouraged to enroll in the industrial education center. Of those who received training, several have been placed in jobs with the assistance of the committee.

During this same period, the Negro community established a special "study-in"—a voluntary program to supplement regular school work and to help youth overcome educational deficiencies. Some 50 students from 11 to 17 years of age have received regular training and as a result, many intend to go to college. These were the same youth who helped to spark street demonstrations which brought mass arrests and racial tensions in the summer of 1963.

A third project which may soon have a strong impact upon Goldsboro is "Operation Bootstrap," a special community effort to wipe out ignorance and poverty. As envisioned by its chief promoter, Mrs. Geneva B. Hamilton, "Bootstrap" would bring school curriculum revision, a clean-up campaign, cooperatives, and increased emphasis upon the arts.

Rocky Mount: Soon after beginning its activities, the Rocky Mount Good Neighbor Council decided that a more basic, formal and long-range plan was necessary for its city. The result was the "Blueprint for Progress," an ex-citing report which has been accepted by the council and other groups as a guideline for present and future action. The report's emphasis is upon better education, expanding job opportunities, and a greater spirit of innovation. Whites and Negroes are expected to benefit equally. In the months following publication of the "Blueprint," the North Carolina Fund selected the Nash-Edgecombe area, of which Rocky Mount is a part, as one of the pilot sites for an anti-poverty drive.

The most recent reports on Negro employment indicate that in the June-December period of 1963, ten industrial firms in Rocky Mount increased their employment from 157 to 245 Negroes. From January to December, nine firms in the retail, clerical, bookkeeping, and teller areas ended their segregated employment and hired from one to three Negroes apiece. Council leaders believe these jobs are less significant, however, than the change in climate, which many feel to be remarkable.

Experiences of Major Employers

A question frequently addressed to the State Good Neighbor Council has concerned the employment practices of major employers and the experiences which they have had in integrating their plants. Generally, the Council has replied, the major employers have led the way and have been pleased with the results.

Western Electric, for instance, has employed on a merit basis for several years. Today Negroes can be found as engineers, draftsmen, chemists, clerk typists, electronic technicians, machinists, inspectors, librarians, and bench production operators. "We give all qualified people the same examination," reports Mr. W. O. Conrad, General Manager of the Greensboro and Burlington plants. "The Negroes' efficiency follows very much the same pattern as the white people."

Another company which has had a merit policy for some time is Reynolds Tobacco Company. Of 12,000 present employees, some 35% are Negroes. Production lines were desegregated in April, 1961. Some Negroes now oversee the production, and others are employed in administrative, supervisory, and clerical positions. Company facilities are also integrated. Officials of Reynolds have stated that their workers have responded well to desegregation. "We got very little kick back," reported one spokesman. "What little there was came from outside the area. The magnificent thing is that there was none from our own employees."

In recent months, Burlington Industries has greatly stepped up its employment of Negroes. Robert B. Lincks, Assistant Personnel Manager, has stated that "Burlington Industries has made progress in every one of our plants in hiring Negroes and upgrading them to our top jobs. We have not discriminated in their favor, but we have been careful in our selection. We have used testing to help us in determining their promotion. Burlington Industries has taken a planned, careful approach and it has been successful."

The Bowman Gray School of Medicine at Wake Forest College also reports satisfactory results from employment of Negroes. Dr. C. C. Carpenter, Dean of the school, has stated, "We have found among our most talented, competent, reliable associates those of the Negro race. We regularly employ competent and qualified Negroes for research assistants, technicians, and similar duties."

Still another area of employment in which merit practices have had successful results is the State's Prison De-

Commitment to Jail: Law and Procedure

(Continued from page 13)

account of expenses" incurred in the custody and transportation of convicted felons to central prison. In such cases as these, since the State Prison Department assumes no responsibility for the prisoners until they are received by the Department, any sheriff or jailer in whose custody such prisoner has been placed for transportation would in all respects be liable for his escape from custody before he was delivered to the State Prison Department.

Rarely nowadays are juveniles or mentally ill or inebriate persons ever taken into the county jails and detained there. But the sheriff is often called upon to take such persons into custody and thereby become responsible for them until a proper disposition has been made by the appropriate court or official. In other words, such persons are rarely *committed* to jail except in cases of extreme emergency, and then only for very short periods of time.[25] Ordinarily, however, there are probation officers available to take custody of juveniles arrested and charged with crime. Similarly, the juvenile judge (clerk of superior court in the majority of counties) will usually order an immediate disposition according to the nature of the offense and other circumstances.[26]

Post-Commitment Procedures: Photographing and Fingerprinting

The popular belief that every person who is for any reason committed to jail must be photographed, fingerprinted, and placed in the "mug book" is erroneous. There are certain restrictions upon the systematic compilation of such a portfolio upon each person committed to jail awaiting trial or hearing, or upon each person convicted of a misdemeanor. The statute[27] provides:

Every chief of police and sheriff in the State of North Carolina is hereby required to take or cause to be taken on forms furnished by this Records Section the fingerprints of *every person convicted of a felony*, and to forward the same immediately by mail to the said Consolidated Records Section —Prison Department. The said officers are hereby required to take the fingerprints of any other person when arrested for a crime when the same is deemed advisable by any. chief of police or sheriff, and forward the same for record to the said Records Section. *No officer, however, shall take the photograph of a person arrested and charged or convicted of a misdemeanor unless such person is* a fugitive from justice, or unless such person is, at the time of arrest, in possession of goods or property reasonably believed by such officer to have been stolen, or unless the officer has reasonable grounds to believe that such person is wanted by the Federal Bureau of Investigation, or the State Bureau of Investigation, or some other law enforcing officer or agency.

Under this statute, sheriffs and chiefs of police are (1) *required* to take the fingerprints of every person convicted of a felony; (2) *may* take the fingerprints of any person arrested for a felony or misdemeanor when, in the opinion of such sheriff or chief of police fingerprinting is advisable; (3) *may* take the photograph of any person convicted of or arrested and charged with a felony, and (4) *may* take the photograph of a person arrested and charged or convicted of a misdemeanor if such person is, at the time of arrest (a) in possession of goods or property reasonably believed by the sheriff or chief of police to have been stolen, or (b) if the sheriff or chief of police has

25. See N.C. Gen. Stat. §§ 122-61 (1964); 110-30 (1960). See also N.C. Gen. Stat. § 110-29(6) (1960) and State v. Coble, 181 N.C. 554, 107 S.E. 132 (1921).

26. N.C. Gen. Stat. §§ 110-29, 110-31 (Supp. 1963).

27. N.C. Gen. Stat. § 148-79 (1964). [Emphasis added.]

---

partment, which has added several Negroes to its staff in recent months. "We have been well pleased with the applicants in general," writes Director George W. Randall. "Of all Negroes employed, it has been necessary to separate only a Unit Superintendent and a Farm Supervisor. Those employments were made about three years ago, before we had improved our screening processes. With the above exceptions, we are pleased to report that the job performance of Negro employees in the North Carolina Prison Department has ranged from good to outstanding. We have found these employees to be dependable, loyal, capable, and conscientious workers."

In the merchandise field, during recent months, many stores have reportedly trained and hired Negroes for the first time. Promotions to non-traditional jobs has also occurred in several areas. To date, according to the North Carolina Merchants' Association, employers have been pleased with the performances and have found little objection by customers. Typical of the employer response is this statement by a variety store manager: "We have asked our managers to adopt a tolerant and understanding attitude on this matter and to seek the opportunity to employ Negroes when good applications are received. Also, it was suggested that they counsel with school principals and other leaders. To date, we have three persons employed as salespeople. They have been well received among other personnel and by our customers."

Conclusions

Although coming from many different areas and telling of different experiences, the reports of these councils and employers have one striking similarity: They all denote a change in the actions and attitudes of many North Carolinians. The polarization of opinion does not seem to be as sharp and distinct as some commentators would suggest, but without a doubt many whites who were formerly unconcerned have adopted a new approach. The conscience of the State has quickened. Employers in nearly every community have opened their doors, some only a crack but some all the way. The Negro response has also been encouraging. For every Negro who has gone through the doors, many others have resolved to train themselves for entrance.

"I believe we have made substantial progress in North Carolina during recent months," states Mr. Coltrane. "Compare our position of a year or two ago with our position today. The Negro has advanced in both employment and education. I am even more pleased with the change which has occurred in the opinions of our people, for this insures us of an opportunity for greater advancement in the future. I do not believe the Civil Rights Act would have been accepted in the manner it has, had this change in opinion not occurred."

Yet, he cautions, "we would not be honest if we failed to recognize that we have just begun and that this is a long-range program."

Obtainment of equal employment opportunities now appears to be the first goal which can be reached down a long, winding road. The voluntary efforts of some elements of the business community and the results which they have had give promise of a growing movement. The equal employment provisions of the Civil Rights Act may also clear the way in some areas. It is evident, however, that the Act will not be effective until a consensus exists within a community. Hence, voluntary work is still needed from community leaders and businessmen.

The leaders of the Good Neighbor program have quickly learned that if their work is to be effective, they must establish bonds of trust with businessmen and must not try to dictate policies. At the same time, the leaders do have a definite point of view upon which the program is based. They are not interested in employment quotas or the employment of people who are unqualified, but they are equally disinterested in attempts to pass off one Negro in the front office as proof of equal employment, or efforts to recruit Negroes only for those super-duper jobs for which there are no qualified whites, or practices of hiring one Negro in order to judge the entire race. The leaders are simply interested in the employment and upgrading of every individual on the basis of merit.

The task of educating Negroes for productive employment often seems to be one of another magnitude. There are signs of progress, but the more obvious signs of our day point again and again to the distressing facts reviewed earlier in this article. Solutions will no doubt require massive efforts. The Good Neighbor program certainly does not have the capacity to eliminate these problems. Its leaders believe, however, that it can reduce some of the difficulties by alerting Negro youth to new job possibilities and by impressing upon them the need for a full education—an education which is not only rich in content but also well directed towards a productive life. Of equal importance, the program can call attention to the conditions of Negro life and appeal for a State-wide effort to raise the living standards of all citizens.

"There is a great deal that all of us working together can do," Coltrane has told many groups around North Carolina. "With the proper co-operation from business, government, and labor; from city, town, and community leaders; from church leaders and forward-looking citizens, we can make the next decade the greatest ever in our desire for equal employment opportunities and better education for all citizens.

"North Carolina," he has said, "has the opportunity to demonstrate to the South, the Nation, and the World both its capacity for orderly change and the extent of its faith in its future. A moment of decision has come for each of us and for our community and State. Challenging opportunities present growth, and I am confident that North Carolina has only begun its growth in our time. The North Carolina dream must become a reality. The words of love, good will, neighborliness, brotherhood, and faith have a common ring that surmounts time and place."

---

reasonable grounds to believe that such person is wanted by some other law enforcement officer or agency, either state or federal. Thus, no officer is ever *required* to take the photograph of any person, irrespective of the crime charged or the nature of the offense of which convicted.

Post-Commitment Procedures:
Health and Sanitary Measures

"All persons confined or imprisoned in any State, county, or city prison or jail shall, within 48 hours after commitment, be examined for venereal diseases by the county physician or other authorized physician. . . ."[28] Boards of county commissioners are authorized to appoint and provide for compensation of a county physician who, where appointed, is responsible for carrying out the provisions of the foregoing section relating to examination and treatment of prisoners for venereal disease.[29] Moreover, authority to make necessary rules and regulations for the purpose of carrying out the provisions of the statute relating to venereal disease is vested in the State Board of Health.[30]

While the requirement that prisoners be examined for venereal disease is mandatory and affects all prisoners confined for forty-eight hours or more, examinations for tuberculosis (and presumably any other disease or malady) appear to be required only when the sheriff, jailer, or other law enforcement officer has reason to suspect a prisoner of being infected. On the other hand, it is expressly provided that "It shall be the duty of every county or city physician or local health director, or other physician responsible for the medical care of city, county, or State prisoners, within his respective jurisdiction, to make a thorough physical examination of *every prisoner* within forty-eight hours after admission of such prisoner. . . ."[31]

There are no further specific requirements for medical examination of prisoners committed to the jails; however, it is within the discretion of the boards of county commissioners to make such rules and regulations in this regard as they deem necessary or advisable. It is generally the practice in this State for jailers to require every prisoner, upon commitment, to bathe, and to provide shaving and haircut facilities for male prisoners and necessary items for personal care of female prisoners. It is incumbent upon every jailer to provide for emergency treatment of any prisoner who becomes ill or injured while in the jail.[32]

Release of Prisoners on Bail

As stated earlier, a necessary component of a valid commitment order is a provision for bail or recognizance. Similarly, arresting officers are required, except in capital cases, to have bail fixed in a reasonable sum. Thus, unless the crime with which the accused is charged is capital, (in which case bail may still be set by a judge of superior court or a Supreme Court Justice) all persons arrested and charged with crime may be allowed bail. In a sense, then, we could say that all persons committed to the jail upon being arrested and charged with crime may be released on bail, and that since it is the duty of the arresting officer to have bail set in a reasonable sum (except in capital cases), the jailer himself is bound only to comply with the terms of the commitment order respecting bail. But just what such terms are

28. N.C. Gen. Stat. § 130-97 (1964).
29. See N.C. Gen. Stat. §§ 130-23, 130-97, 130-101 (1964).
30. N.C. Gen. Stat. § 130-99 (1964).

31. N.C. Gen. Stat. § 130-121 (1964).

32. See Spicer v. Williamson, 191 N.C. 487, 132 S.E. 291 (1926).

THIS MONTH AT THE INSTITUTE

often presents a difficult question, particularly with regard to what is meant by "fix" and "take," and whether they mean in every case that bail *fixed* by one official may be *taken* by another.

The first provision[33] in the statutes setting out the officers who are authorized to take bail states:

Officers before whom person [sic] charged with crime, but who have not been committed to prison by an authorized magistrate, may be brought, have power to fix and take bail as follows:
(1) Any justice of the Supreme Court, or a judge of superior court, in all cases.
(2) Any clerk of the superior court, any justice of the peace, any chief magistrate of any incorporated city or town, or any person authorized to issue warrants of arrest, in all cases of misdemeanor, and in all cases of felony not capital.

Although the title of this section includes only "officers authorized to take bail," it is clear that all officers listed may fix the amount of bail in any case, and then take such bail or recognizance and release the defendant. Thus, if the defendant is taken before any of the listed officials before he is taken to jail, and is able to meet bail requirements as fixed by such official, he never gets to jail. But if the defendant is unable to meet the bail requirements at the time of his appearance before such official, he then goes to jail, apparently to remain there until he is able to provide the requisite bail.

The next section[34] in the article

entitled *Bail* achieves a result which is for all effects and purposes similar to the one quoted above. It provides:

Officers authorized to take bail, after imprisonment.—Any justice of the Supreme Court or any judge of a superior court has power to fix and take bail for persons committed to prison charged with crime in all cases; any justice of the peace, any chief magistrate of any incorporated city or town, or any person authorized to issue warrants of arrest has the same power in all cases where the punishment is not capital.

Here, if a person has been committed to jail before he has had a hearing, any of the same officers listed in G.S. 15-102 may fix and take bail, limited only by the provision relating to capital offenses. Therefore, it matters not whether bail is fixed before or after the defendant is imprisoned in the jail; he is still entitled to have bail fixed. And under the last section quoted above, any officer who fixes bail may also take it, thereby avoiding the return of such defendant to the jail though he had been there pending the hearing at which bail was fixed and taken. But this still leaves us with another question in any case where bail is neither fixed nor taken by the officer before whom the defendant is taken for a hearing.

The implication in the principal commitment statute[35] is that the sheriff or jailer may fix and take bail in such cases. However, in view of the particular language of the foregoing statutes and another section in the article entitled *Bail*, it is not perfectly clear whether a sheriff or jailer may ever *fix* bail. Nevertheless,

it is expressly provided:[36]

When any sheriff or his deputy arrests the body of any person, in consequence of the writ of capias issued to him by the clerk of a court of record on an indictment found, the sheriff or deputy, if the crime is bailable, shall recognize the offender, and take sufficient bail in the nature of a recognizance for his appearing at the next succeeding court of the county where he ought to answer, which recognizance shall be returned with the capias; and the sheriff shall in no case become bail himself. . . .

This section speaks of a recognizance taken after arrest on a *capias*, and not of the fixing and taking of bail from a person arrested on a warrant. Strictly construed, it would not permit a sheriff to take recognizance from any person arrested on any process except a *capias* issued after an indictment had been found against such person.

But there is still another statute[37] which both clarifies and confuses this issue. It states:

If any person for want of bail shall be lawfully committed to jail at any time before final judgment, the sheriff or other officer having him in custody, may take sufficient justified bail and discharge him; and the bail bond shall be reguarded, in every respect, as other bail bonds, and shall be returned and sued on in like manner; and the officer taking it shall make special return thereof with the bond, at the first court which is held after it is taken.

This section clarifies the issue concerning whether a sheriff or jailer may *take* bail and release a prisoner who has been lawfully committed after having had bail *fixed*, but being unable at that time to provide it. But is the language "take sufficient justified bail and discharge him" intended to mean that the sheriff may *fix* the bail in such cases? This is confusing.

A strict interpretation of the entire article which, incidentally, has not been the subject of thorough interpretation by the Court, leads to these conclusions: (1) a sheriff or jailer may not *fix* bail except in cases of arrest upon a *capias* issued on an indictment found against some person; (2) a sheriff or jailer may *take*

---

33. N.C. Gen. Stat. § 15-102 (Supp. 1963).
34. N.C. Gen. Stat. § 15-103 (Supp. 1963)

35. N.C. Gen. Stat. § 15-125 (1953).

36. N.C. Gen. Stat. § 15-107 (Supp. 1963).
37. N.C. Gen. Stat. § 15-108 (1953).

What Price Traffic Safety?

(Continued from page 7)

courts. Under proposed court reform certain state district judges in larger communities might be able to specialize in traffic cases. Obviously, much time and thought have been, and are being, given to traffic safety needs, and things are stirring.

The theme of safe driving has constantly sounded in newspapers, on radio, television and films and from speakers' platforms throughout the state. There has been no lack of planning or effort to make driving safe on our highways and no reason for lack of awareness of either the problem or the toll.

Why then are the results so frustrating? Certain things may be said.

Dr. James H. Grout illustrates a point on "Vision Testing' during the AAMVA-Institute of Government Driver License School.

1. The problem is so complex as to defy panaceas and no quick nor easy solutions should be expected.
2. It is likely to get worse as the number of drivers and the volume of motor traffic and road complexes expand with the population. (This is a two-way street. If the death and accident figures go higher, the fact of more cars, roads, drivers and miles travelled helps explain and mitigate the increase.)
3. There is neither time nor reason for despair. The problem will continue. So will pressures to meet it. We might ask ourselves some questions:
   a. What would be the death, injury and property toll if we had none of these programs?
   b. Does not the dedication of increasing numbers of able public officials and private citizens to traffic safety research and progress suggest that not only something is being done about the existence of widespread faith that more can be done and *must* be done?
   c. Is there not a need for more rather than less coordinated planning in traffic safety?

This century has brought breakthroughs in so many fields (in addition to the one which resulted in the invention of that great boon, the motor

vehicle) that who is to say there will be no breakthroughs to help solve the traffic problem—provided the present growing impetus in research and programs is carried on with determination?

That breakthrough could come in the eventual adoption of other means of transportation which could take some of the load off our streets and highways. It could come in the form of safety devices and features in motor vehicles and new protections for the drivers. It could come in more effective means of communicating with drivers and instilling safe driving habits. It could come with better enforcement techniques and processes and advanced methods for finding and removing problem drivers from our highways. It may come from appropriate changes in our courts system and through developments in driver education and driver improvement. It could come from a combination of these and other factors. If this is no time to fool ourselves as to the magnitude of the problem, neither is it a time for pause in the safety effort. For so long as mass transportation is vital to our growing industrial and travelling society, no answer is possible which does not recognize at once the complex of legal, medical, psychological, economic and social relationships and implications which underlie and underscore the problem and seek the best available professional skills to make for safer use of potentially lethal weapons on our streets and highways through the spread of public and personal responsibility. No driver rides alone; each is his brother's keeper.

—Elmer Oettinger

---

bail from any person for whom bail has been fixed by an authorized officer, but who was, at the time bail was fixed, unable to provide it; (3) any officer listed in G.S. 15-102 and 15-103 may *fix* and *take* bail, either before or after the defendant has been committed to jail, and (4) all persons charged with crime less than capital are entitled to have bail fixed before commitment to jail, and those who are committed to jail without bail upon being charged with a capital crime are entitled, upon a petition for a writ of *habeas corpus*, to a hearing

before a superior court judge or Supreme Court Justice to determine whether or not they may be admitted to bail.[38]

As to the commitment order required by G.S. 15-125, and particularly with respect to the portion concerning bail or recognizance, it seems that there may be a widespread practice in this State of the use of printed forms upon which blank spaces are left to be filled out by arresting officers and jailers. As stated earlier,

38. See State v. Herndon, 107 N.C. 934, 12 S.E. 268 (1890).

a verbal commitment order is no good. Moreover, in 1942, in response to a question posed by an officer of the State Highway Patrol, the Attorney General in a lengthy opinion condemned the use of printed forms with blanks left for use by officers. The Attorney General said:

Obviously, the issuance of a commitment is a judicial act which cannot be delegated. I am of the opinion that the practice of committing prisoners on commitments completed by the officers

(Continued inside back cover)

● NOTES FROM . . .

CITIES AND COUNTIES

A Civil Aeronautics Board ruling has apparently opened the way for construction of an airport between *Rocky Mount* and *Wilson*. A group of eastern Tar Heel communities — *Greenville, Washington, Farmville, Williamston, Snow Hill,* and the counties of *Pitt, Beaufort, Martin* and *Greene* — had challenged the CAB's decision to continue airline services at present airports in Rocky Mount, *Kinston,* Greenville, *Goldsboro* and Wilson. In a 3-2 vote, the CAB denied the reconsideration petition.

＊   ＊   ＊

The Federal Aviation Agency in its National Airport Plan for 1965-70 has recommended 727 new landing facilities across the nation. Listed in the idealized plan are *Bryson City, Charlotte, Concord, Durham, Elkin, Erwin, Franklin, Greensboro-High Point, Henderson, Lexington, Lincolnton, Louisburg, Monroe, Mooresville, Reidsville, Rocky Mount, Roxboro, Rutherfordton, Smithfield, Taylorsville, Waynesville, West Jefferson* and *Williamston.*

Steady progress has been reported by the *Onslow* County-*Jacksonville* Airport Commission in preparing the area's case for a commercial airport at a CAB hearing in December.

＊   ＊   ＊

Person County commissioners have agreed to participate in financing an engineering study for a proposed *Roxboro*-Person County airport.

＊   ＊   ＊

Area Redevelopment

Chowan County has been removed from the status of area redevelopment area, according to the U. S. Department of Labor. Economic development has improved along with employment and the pattern seems likely to continue.

Central Business District

Plexiglass canopies now line the main drag in *Varina.* The dramatic face-lifting, designed to counter the shopping center influence on buyers, is expected to extend into the *Fuquay* business district.

＊   ＊   ＊

Planners have suggested a shopper's pedestrian mall for *Whiteville's* Madison Street. This improvement to the central business district, according to the North Carolina Division of Community Planning, would boost Whiteville's potential as a shopping center for the surrounding rural area.

＊   ＊   ＊

A second downtown plaza has been recommended for *Raleigh.* The first is under construction on Exchange Street and the second would be located on Market Street.

＊

Education

Martin County's boards of education and commissioners have tentatively made plans to hold a $3,000,000 school bond issue vote early in 1965.

＊   ＊   ＊

Dallas has annexed *Gaston* College, effective November 1, but it won't be for long. Present plan is to introduce a bill in the state legislature which would remove the college from city incorporation but leave it encircled by Dallas. A foot wide buffer zone will be established on the south and west sides.

＊   ＊   ＊

Rutherford County voters approved a community college with an 18 to one vote majority. The site in the Oakland community has been okayed and final approval for the school has come from the State department of community colleges.

＊   ＊   ＊

Dare County commissioners have adopted a resolution to accept the

$330,000 indebtedness of the *Manteo* and *Kitty Hawk* school districts. Voters will decide the issue this month.

＊   ＊   ＊

Chapel Hill has launched a unique pre-technical program of studies in health occupations as part of its senior high school curriculum. The three-year program is set up for about 30 pupils beginning in the 10th grade. The program will function in cooperation with North Carolina Memorial Hospital and has resulted in similar setups in five other Tar Heel school systems.

＊   ＊   ＊

Moore County's commissioners have agreed to issue the full $1 million worth of county bonds approved by voters a year ago for the Sandhills Community College. The State will add a supplementary $500,000 for construction of the college.

＊   ＊   ＊

Goldsboro's Wayne Technical Institute and the *Sampson* County Board of Education have entered into a joint adult education project in the Sampson schools. High school diplomas will be the goal of the drop-outs enrolled.

＊   ＊   ＊

Asheboro is trying a novel three-year program designed to up-grade the effectiveness of teaching in the academic areas of the systems secondary schools. Eight local firms contributed $37,500 to finance the Asheboro Plan which places exceptionally talented teachers in key positions as directors of instruction in five academic areas.

＊

Elections

Plans to reshape and rename *Winston-Salem's* wards got a unanimous favorable vote from the Board of Aldermen and now need only approval of the General Assembly to give the city its first major ward

22

realignment since 1949.

Iredell, Robeson and Madison were among the counties undertaking a complete new voter registration prior to the November 3 elections.

Fire Prevention
Catawba County's new fire communications system, installed in 13 fire departments, has received top ratings from the Fire and Rescue Division of the North Carolina Department of Insurance.

A second fire station has opened in Dunn. One of the main reasons for its construction was to protect interests in the western sector of the city, separated by a railroad from the main fire station.

Highways and Streets
Beaufort town commissioners have endorsed a resolution reminding the State Highway Commission of the need for a high-level bridge across Bogue Sound to Bogue Banks. Morehead City aldermen had previously endorsed the resolution.

Housing
Plymouth's city council has voted to establish a Public Housing Authority. The community will ask for a 50-unit housing program for low-income families.

Contracts have been let for construction of 120 units of low-rent housing for the Sanford Housing Authority.

Since the activation of the Hickory Substandard Housing Ordinance in February, 1963, a total of 131 substandard houses have been demolished. In addition 61 have been repaired, or are in the process of repair.

Municipal Buildings
Preliminary courthouse annex plans have been approved in Durham County. Parking facilities have been eliminated from the plan but the cost is still $150,000 more than expected.

Formal dedication of Roxboro's new municipal building took place in September.

Contracts have been let in Kernersville for construction of a new town hall. The plan has been drawn to in-

clude future enlargements and a possible second story.

Planning
A 123-page guidebook to promote and coordinate development of the Durham-Chapel Hill-Raleigh area has been given an official sendoff by the Research Triangle Regional Planning Commission. The "compass" for the metropolitan Triangle area points the direction for an expected population boom — more than 200,000 during the next 16 years.

Smaller communities in the area— Carrboro, Hillsboro, Cary, Wendell, Creedmoor, Rougemont, Apex and Fuquay-Varina — are also included in the report.

FORFEITED FINES FAN FLAMES
A large number of unpaid parking tickets went up in smoke in Murfreesboro.

Occasion for the cremation was the elevation of Raymond Mann to the top spot on the police force when Chief W. T. Liverman resigned after 19 years of service. Town commissioners decided to let Chief Mann begin his administration with a clean slate — and a more rigid policy of parking violation enforcement.

Public Health
Henderson County residents are being served by an enlarged Margaret R. Pardee Memorial Hospital. Sixty-nine beds were added to the hospital which is valued at three and a half million dollars.

Halifax commissioners are considering establishing a full-time mental health clinic for the county. State, federal and county funds would be used to construct the clinic and State funds would be used in making up the operational budget.

Four years after Carteret voters approved a bond issue for a county hospital the project has received approval to use State and federal funds. The hospital will be built at Camp Glenn near Morehead City.

Public Libraries
Elkin's public library has officially been accepted as a member of the Northwest Regional Library Association.

Forest City's $90,000 Mooneyham Public Library was dedicated in mid-October. The building is the 62nd new library building dedicated since 1950 in North Carolina and the fifth this year.

To augment town, county and federal funds available for construction of the proposed Johnston County-Smithfield Public Library, a $15,000 fund-raising campaign has been launched on a popular level.

An addition to increase High Point's floor space by 32 percent should be ready for spring occupancy. The addition will cost $100,000.

Recreation
Winston-Salem voters turned out in record numbers — 15,373 — to support by a two-to-one ratio a referendum to support the city's recreation program. Two propositions were accepted: use of up to 10 cents in tax money for recreation funds and expenditure of $1 million for parks and pools.

Oakboro joins the roster of Tar Heel communities using surplus jet fighters in community recreation areas.

A daily year-round program for senior citizens is being planned at the Greensboro Community Center. The city has some 7,000 residents over age 65 and the number is expected to increase sharply each year.

Sanitation
Burnsville voters authorized the issuance of $175,000 in bonds for construction of a new sewage disposal facility. The vote was 200 to eight.

Catawba has a new $100,000 sewage treatment plant which operates by

(Continued inside back cover)

• BOOK REVIEWS •

NORTH CAROLINA AND THE NEGRO, published by the North Carolina Mayors' Co-Operating Committee; edited by Capus M. Waynick, John C. Brooks, and Elsie W. Pitts. The State College Print Shop, Raleigh, North Carolina, 1964. 309 pp.

As Mayor Brookshire says in his preface, the North Carolina Mayors' Co-Operating Committee was organized in July, 1963, in response to Governor Sanford's belief that the handling of the race problem should rest largely with local government and businessmen. The merit of this approach is made clear in this book which recounts the progress made by biracial committees, human relations committees, and Good Neighbor Councils in fifty-five cities and towns across the state from Asheville to Elizabeth City.

The history of the Negro protest movement is briefly traced and is followed by an objective analysis of how each of the towns and cities covered have responded to what Mayor Grabarek of Durham has said to be not "a problem — but an opportunity." Success in adjustment of differences has varied from community to community, but perhaps more importantly, lines of communication — a necessary element for progress in this area — have been maintained in almost all.

This book should be useful to any community or citizen who wishes to see these lines of communication develop or continue in order to promote peaceful and desirable adjustments of racial differences. In addition to the account of how other communities have acted, there are helpful sections telling how to go about setting up a biracial council and suggesting appropriate ways and means of action. (See box below.)

The book is richly illustrated with many photographs recording the history of the desegregation movement in North Carolina. Also, there is an excellent bibliography of material in the race relations field. This work deserves praise both as a record of a significant period in North Carolina history and as a useful handbook for the solution of immediate problems.

Gapus M. Waynick is special consultant to the Governor on race relations; John C. Brooks is administrator of the North Carolina Mayors' Co-Operating Committee; and Elsie W. Pitts is recording secretary for the North Carolina Mayor's Co-Operating Committee.

North Carolina and the Negro is available through the North Carolina Mayors' Co-operating Committe, P. O. Box 2539, Raleigh. The paperback price is $2; clothbound, $3.

THE WARREN REPORT: REPORT ON THE PRESIDENT'S COMMISSION ON THE ASSASSINATION OF PRESIDENT JOHN F. KENNEDY. United States Government Printing Office, 1964. 336 pages. $3.00. (As the Associated Press Printing: $1.50.)

The best way to know and fully understand the evidence on which the Warren Commission based its findings on the assassination of President John F. Kennedy is to read the official Warren Report. The information, compiled and presented through eight chapters and eighteen appendices, provides a compelling basis and background for the summary and conclusions of the Commission which are stated in Chapter 1. The Commission's criticism of the press and local and federal law enforcement agencies calls for thoughtful attention and appropriate action. The volume itself is testimony to careful and thoroughgoing research and investigation procedures.

Guidelines in Community Relations *

By STANFORD R. BROOKSHIRE

1. Recognition and acceptance of inevitability of changes in our long existing social and economic patterns are necessary. Negroes have made it abundantly clear that they are no longer willing to accept indignities and disadvantages of second-class citizenship.
2. Responsibility of each community is to seek and to find its own solutions.
3. Choice is clearly between accepting changes and using them constructively for community betterment or resisting changes with disastrous results.
4. Of the three measures thus far employed, (1) legal, (2) protest actions, and (3) biracial co-operation, the last has produced the best and perhaps the most lasting results in the preservation of racial harmony, progress, and prosperity.
5. Biracial councils carefully constructed of top leadership of both races to population ratio, in regular meetings, can (it has been proved) develop mutual understanding, promote good will and develop co-operation.
6. It is important to involve total community leadership—business, civic, and church.
7. Initiative should originate with local government, which should remove all unconstitutional ordinances and offer employment to all citizens on merit basis, without favor or discrimination.
8. Social conscience, civic pride, and economic considerations can make proper climate for change.
9. Progress can be made only when prejudice gives way to reason, animosities to good will, apathy to action.
10. We must emphasize the importance of equating responsibility as a two-way street.
11. Emphasis on full utilization of human resources is essential. People are either ain asset or a liability to their community.
12. Discrimination based on color is morally and legally wrong and economically unsound.
13. Constructive effort through removal of inequalities and providing educational and economic opportunities without bias is a basic attack on poverty and crime.
14. There must be conversion of problems to opportunities to build better communities, a better nation, a better world.

* Reprinted, with permission, from *North Carolina and the Negro.*

COMMUNICATIONS AND POLITICAL DEVELOPMENT. Edited by Lucian W. Pye. Princeton University Press, 1963. 381 pages.

This volume establishes clear and vital links between communications and political development in the modern world. The first in a series of studies under a grant from the Ford Foundation, the book grew out of papers prepared for a 1961 conference on Communication and Political Development. Chapters include "Communcation Development and the Development Process" by Wilbur Schramm, "Mass Media and Political Socialization: The Role of Patterns of Communication" by Herbert Hyman, and "Communications and Civic Training in Transitional Societies." There are chapters relating to communications policies and patterns as related to government in such countries as Thailand, Turkey, and Communist China. The book is especially valuable to those interested in the relationship and influence of communications to politics and government.

RECENT BOOKS ON GOVERNMENT

STATE GOVERNMENT AND TRANSITION: REFORMS OF THE LEADER ADMINISTRATION, 1959. By Reed M. Smith. Philadelphia: University of Pennsylvania Press, 1963. 309 pages.

THE CONGRESSMAN: HIS WORK AS HE SEES IT. By Charles L. Clapp. Washington: The Bookings Institution, 1963. 452 pages. $6.00.

THE DEADLOCK OF DEMOCRACY: FOUR-PARTY POLITICS IN AMERICA. By James MacGregor Burns. Prentice-Hall, Inc., 1963. 378 pages.

PUBLIC AUTHORITIES, SPECIAL DISTRICTS AND LOCAL GOVERNMENT. By Robert G. Smith. Washington: National Association of Counties Research Foundation, 1964. 225 pages.

LIBERTY IN THE BALANCE: CURRENT ISSUES IN CIVIL LIBERTIES. By H. Frank Way, Jr. New York: McGraw-Hill, 1964. 136 pages.

Commitment to Jail

(Continued from page 21)

after having been signed in blank by a magistrate without an examination of the prisoner is clearly unlawful and subject to great abuse. . . .[39]

However, in the same opinion the Attorney General went further to say, with respect to situations where the arresting officer cannot, at the time of arrest, take the accused person before a magistrate, that such persons should be committed to jail by the arresting officer until they can be taken before a magistrate.

Most of the printed forms examined by the author contain appropriate spaces and printed matter which, when completed, go to make up a valid commitment order as contemplated by G.S. 15-125, including the provisions for bail or recognizance. Thus, in keeping with the provisions of G.S. 15-108 relating to the taking of bail by the sheriff, it seems that if the committing magistrate completes the form and thereon directs the sheriff to take bail in a specified sum, if the accused person has had a hearing before such magistrate the entire procedure is valid. This is true even though the blank spaces on the form left for acknowledgment of bail or sureties are completed at the jail instead of before the magistrate or judge who set bail.

Up to this point we have been discussing the taking of bail from persons charged with crime—not from persons convicted of crime. Moreover, we have not concerned ourselves in this paper with arrest and commitment to bail of *civil* defendants. Since the latter subject is taken up in detail in a recent publication,[40] no mention will be made of it here. As to the right of persons to bail who have been convicted and are awaiting appeals, there are specific statutory provisions which ought to be mentioned.

One statute[41] gives any person convicted of a misdemeanor or a noncapital felony the right to give bail

39. *Biennial Report of the Attorney General,* Vol. 27 p. 385 (1942-1944).
40. See Harper, *North Carolina Sheriffs' Manual,* Institute of Government (1964), Ch. IV.
41. N.C. Gen. Stat. § 15-183 (Supp. 1963).

pending an appeal. This right is absolute, with respect to having bail set in some amount, except as to those persons who are sentenced to death (who may not be released on bail) and those who are convicted of capital offenses and sentenced to life imprisonment, in which case whether or not they may be committed to bail pending the outcome of their appeals lies solely within the discretion of the trial court. The other statute[42] specifically provides that the release on bail of a person convicted and sentenced does not operate to vacate the judgment or sentence, but acts only as a stay of execution of the sentence pending the outcome of the appeal.

42. N.C. Gen. Stat. § 15-184 (Supp. 1963).

Notes from Cities and Counties

(Continued from page 23)

pressuring air into the water. The creation of Lake Norman necessitated the change.

* *

Manteo has been told by the State Division of Steam Sanitation that it must have a new sewage disposal system costing in the neighborhood of $300,000. Federal aid wil be sought for the project.

* *

Princeton's new lagoon type sewage treatment plant replaces a system in operation for 30 years. The facility is the last of improvements paid for by a $140,000 bond issue.

* *

Urban Renewal

A bond issue to enable *Whiteville* to pay its one-quarter share of a proposed urban renewal program has been suggested by the town council. The vote will likely be held early in 1965 and would be for $300,000.

How Population . . . May Affect Water Resources

(Continued from page 10)

neither serious conflicts among water users nor unusual demands for water resources development, and may not do so within present planning horizons.

All photographs and map on page 9 by Charles Nakamura. Design by Lynn Deal. Excerpt on page 24 from the book North Carolina and the Negro reprinted with permission of the North Carolina Mayors' Co-operating Committee.

Flavor that goes with fun...

Modern filter here ▶ ◀ Filter-Blend up front

Winston is the filter cigarette with flavor...the best flavor in filter smoking.
Change to Winston...America's largest-selling filter cigarette. by far!

Winston tastes good...like a cigarette should!